LOST MINES
& BURIED TREASURES
ALONG THE OLD FRONTIER

P. O. Box 36 Marceline, Missouri 64658
Telephone (816) 376-3523

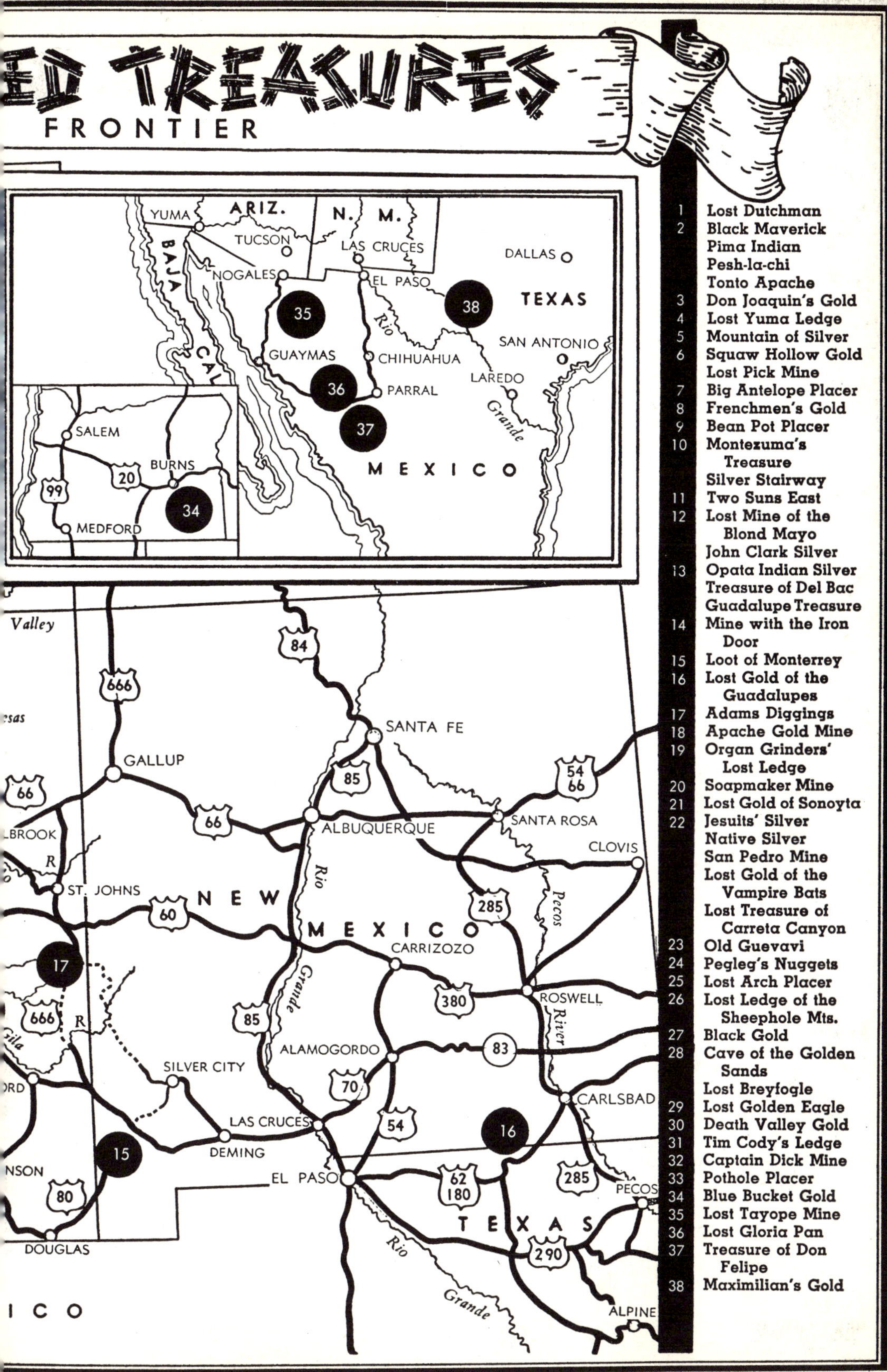

ED TREASURES
FRONTIER
YUMA
ARIZ.
N. M.
TUCSON
LAS CRUCES
DALLAS
BAJA
NOGALES
EL PASO
35
38
TEXAS
Rio
SAN ANTONIO
GUAYMAS
CHIHUAHUA
CAL
LAREDO
36
PARRAL
37
Grande
SALEM
MEXICO
BURNS
20
99
34
MEDFORD
Valley
84
666
sas
SANTA FE
GALLUP
85
54
66
66
66
SANTA ROSA
ALBUQUERQUE
LBROOK
CLOVIS
R
Rio
ST. JOHNS
NEW
285
Pecos
60
MEXICO
CARRIZOZO
17
Grande
ROSWELL
380
666
R
85
River
Gila
ALAMOGORDO
83
SILVER CITY
RD
70
CARLSBAD
LAS CRUCES
54
16
15
DEMING
NSON
EL PASO
62
180
285
PECOS
80
TEXAS
290
DOUGLAS
Rio
Grande
ALPINE
ICO
1 Lost Dutchman
2 Black Maverick
Pima Indian
Pesh-la-chi
Tonto Apache
3 Don Joaquin's Gold
4 Lost Yuma Ledge
5 Mountain of Silver
6 Squaw Hollow Gold
Lost Pick Mine
7 Big Antelope Placer
8 Frenchmen's Gold
9 Bean Pot Placer
10 Montezuma's Treasure
Silver Stairway
11 Two Suns East
12 Lost Mine of the Blond Mayo
John Clark Silver
13 Opata Indian Silver
Treasure of Del Bac
Guadalupe Treasure
14 Mine with the Iron Door
15 Loot of Monterrey
16 Lost Gold of the Guadalupes
17 Adams Diggings
18 Apache Gold Mine
19 Organ Grinders' Lost Ledge
20 Soapmaker Mine
21 Lost Gold of Sonoyta
22 Jesuits' Silver
Native Silver
San Pedro Mine
Lost Gold of the Vampire Bats
Lost Treasure of Carreta Canyon
23 Old Guevavi
24 Pegleg's Nuggets
25 Lost Arch Placer
26 Lost Ledge of the Sheephole Mts.
27 Black Gold
28 Cave of the Golden Sands
Lost Breyfogle
29 Lost Golden Eagle
30 Death Valley Gold
31 Tim Cody's Ledge
32 Captain Dick Mine
33 Pothole Placer
34 Blue Bucket Gold
35 Lost Tayope Mine
36 Lost Gloria Pan
37 Treasure of Don Felipe
38 Maximilian's Gold

LOST MINES
& BURIED TREASURES
ALONG THE OLD FRONTIER

By JOHN D. MITCHELL

Illustrations by John Hansen
Maps and Titles by Margaret Gerke

GLORIETA, NEW MEXICO · 87535

Desert Press, Inc.
1953
Reprinted by Permission 1970
Desert Magazine
Palm Desert, Calif.

First edition from which this edition was
reproduced was supplied by

FRED ROSENSTOCK, Books,
1228 East Colfax Avenue
Denver, Colo. 80218

A RIO GRANDE CLASSIC
First published in 1954

LIBRARY OF CONGRESS CARD CATALOG
77-121730

ISBN 87380-060-5

1970

GLORIETA, NEW MEXICO · 87535

PUBLISHER'S PREFACE

Earlier this year we published *Lost Mines of the Great Southwest* (first published in 1933) by the author of this book. As is often the case on occasional book writers, we could find out precious little about John D. Mitchell from the usual historical sources. We found practically nothing by press time, so we went with what we had. Shortly afterwards, we discovered he had written a second dandy little book entitled *Lost Mines and Buried Treasures Along the Old Frontier,* first published in 1954 by the Desert Magazine Press at Palm Desert, California.

Now 1954 is not so far from 1970 as is 1933. We picked up the telephone and called our friends (Bill Knyvett and Jack Pepper) at Desert Magazine headquarters (they sell our books). We chatted with Bill, who readily gave us permission to bring the book back into print. The problem then was to find a first edition to work with--they had none at Desert Magazine.

We happened shortly afterward, then, to be talking on the phone with our great and good rare book friend in Denver, Fred Rosenstock. I mentioned that we were planning on reprinting the other Mitchell title as soon as we could locate a first edition to work from. Fred thought he had a copy, he said, and if he did, he would lend it to us. He did have a copy, and in a few days we received in the mail a perfect mint copy in original dust wrapper. And what do you know? There, on the jacket flap, was the following copy verbatim. It isn't really very informative insofar as author Mitchell goes, but aside from the fragment we inserted in *Lost Mines of the Great Southwest,* this is all we have and all we have been able to find. Mitchell was apparently living at Arivaca, Ariz., in 1954, but our inquiries there in 1970 revealed no one who had ever heard of old John D. Mitchell.

". . .John D. Mitchell's acquaintance with the legendary and historical lost mines of the Southwest was acquired through a long life-time of association with mines and mining men.

"He came west from his birthplace at Louisville, Kentucky, while he was still a youth. He crossed the snow-capped Rockies and was attracted to one after another of the mining camps, many of which were in their peak of production in the early part of the present century.

"Gradually he acquired a knowledge of ores, and of mining methods, and his quest for precious metal has taken him to Alaska and into Old Mexico. But always he returned to prospect the mountains and arroyos of the desert Southwest.

"Among mining men and pioneers of the old frontier the conversation invariably turned to the stories of fabulously rich lodes and placer fields which had been discovered and then lost, and to the treasures which the Jesuit and Franciscan padres were reported to have accumulated and stored in underground vaults. He felt that the historical records to which he had access lent considerable credence to some of these lost treasure tales, and he has spent weeks and months between mining ventures tracing the sources of many of these rumors, and in actual search for gold.

"Thanks to a retentive memory, he has been able to pass along to a new generation of gold-seekers much of the information as it came to him, in many instances from old-timers who confided in him only because they regarded him as one of themselves.

"John Mitchell believes implicitly in the truth of the tales he has related in this book, and is confident that sooner or later many of these treasures will be re-discovered.

"In recent years his mining headquarters have been at Arivaca, Arizona, in the heart of the region where many of his lost treasure tales are based."

Whoever wrote that jacket flap copy did a good job of describing the book, for the roaring old tales gallop from lost gold mines to hidden treasures cover to cover. We especially like the idea of the map on the front endsheets which shows the approximate location of all the treasures he so vividly describes. Surely, one thinks, if a searcher can get that close, one should make the grade sooner or later. And for those who are a little more literal minded, we obtained from the Arizona Pioneers' Historical Society a negative for a "Mining and Scientific Press Supplement," (they own the original map) and we have printed and inserted that map at the back of this book as a frame-of-reference foldout. It is more specific, and probably more informative, than the map at the front. The map is c. 1881.

In passing, the reader might take note of the advertisements on the map. We left them on there purposely, for they reflect authentically a moment of time in the marvelous history of Western America.

Really, those who visit the great Southwest on a treasure hunt need both this book and *Lost Mines of the Great Southwest*, for the two complement and supplement each other. With both books giving directions for different mines, with all of them centered on Arizona, southern California and western New Nexico, how can the ambitious reader prospect and miss? A word of warning, though. *Respect that desert!* The dry country is beautiful, even marvelous, but the tenderfoot who underestimates that cascade of sunshine or overestimates his own capacities is sure to find trouble sooner than treasure.

Lost Mines and Buried Treasures along the Old Frontier is our 55th Beautiful Rio Grande Classic, and we think any reader of any age will enjoy it tremendously. And if you do like it, you will then also appreciate equally some of our other titles, like *Black Range Tales* (by James A. McKenna), *Tombstone's Yesterday* (by Lorenzo Walters) and *Helldorado* (by William Breakenridge). They're all great books about a great country and a great time; they're the kind of books that make us older types slap a thigh and mutter: ". . .Git for home, Bruno! Gad, that was a good book!"

Robert B. McCoy

La Casa Escuela
Glorieta, N.M.
July 1970

Pegleg Smith was a trapper —one of the Mountain Men who came into the West 100 years ago and grub-staked their explorations with beaver pelts.

LOST MINES
& BURIED TREASURES
ALONG THE OLD FRONTIER

By JOHN D. MITCHELL

Illustrations by John Hansen
Maps and Titles by Margaret Gerke

DESERT MAGAZINE PRESS
Palm Desert, California

Composed and printed at Palm Desert, California
by the Desert Magazine Press

PREFACE

THE SEARCH for lost mines and buried treasure has ever intrigued mankind and for ages has worn the glamor of legend and romantic mystery. For centuries treasure seekers have searched for the buried chests of Treasure Island, for the Alhambra of Old Granada with its secret caves filled with gold and jewels, for the gems and golden doubloons of lost pirate loot, shipwrecked treasure and buried booty.

One of the latest chapters in the saga of lost riches was written in Mexico and the great American Southwest — a chapter filled with the stories of the Spanish Conquistadores, the Jesuit priests, pioneers, Indians, old-time miners and prospectors who lived in and traveled this vast and desolate land.

The Toltec and Aztec Indians of Mexico understood the mining and smelting of gold and silver and used these precious metals for ornaments, shields, household utensils and religious relics. When the Conquistadores began their triumphal conquest of Mexico, these Indian peoples buried what treasures they could, to prevent them from falling into Spanish hands. With the tribes' eventual destruction, the secret burial places were lost.

Some of the great treasures which the invaders did appropriate also were lost later, buried for safekeeping when the rigors of travel demanded it, or lost when an engagement turned against the Spaniards and the white men were routed. In many instances, the Jesuit priests who followed the Conquistadores established their missions in the Aztec mining centers. Rich mines were opened near the missions, both in

Mexico and in southern Arizona where Papago, Pima and Opata neophytes prospected the hills for precious ore. The Jesuits stored up great wealth from the operation of these mines. According to royal decree, one-fifth of all the bullion recovered was due the Spanish king. Then in 1767 came the edict from Charles III expelling the Jesuit priests from the New World.

The Jesuits undoubtedly foresaw the possibility that they might not be able to carry with them the rich mission treasures, and they buried them in secret caves, underground vaults and other hiding places which were sealed until they could reclaim their riches in safety.

They never returned. Fleeing to the coast and the ships which would return them to Europe, some were killed by hostile Indians. Others perished from the rigors of the long overland journey to the sea. Their treasures remained buried—and lost.

Indians periodically threatened the mission wealth. In the bloody Pima revolt of 1751 and in various other uprisings both before the Jesuits left and after their successors, the Franciscans, took over mission operations, the treasures were buried for security—and sometimes they were never recovered.

Although many of the Southwest's lost mines were bequeathed by the Spanish missionaries, others were left by pioneers who, anxious to reach the settlements and rich farmlands of Oregon and coastal California, were too fearful of the desert to remain and work the deposits they had discovered. In many instances the emigrants—farmers and not mining men—did not recognize the value of rich gold nuggets or yellow-flecked gravel.

Many prospectors—among them Pegleg Smith, Tim Cody, Alkali Jones and the Dutchman, Jacob Walz—also lost bonanza strikes. One small gold-rich gulch is easily lost in the maze of desert mountain canyons. Lack of water in the desert country adds to the difficulty of prospecting and of mining rich lodes once found.

That the stories in this book have an authentic background is proven by history. The fact that the old mines and treasures referred to have not been re-located has not prevented the author from giving important details as to their value and general location. Many of the details have been taken from original Spanish documents and old church records, from the words of old Indians whose ancestors had worked in the mines and of old-timers who themselves had lost once-in-a-lifetime strikes or knew prospectors who had.

The author has spent many years in the desert mountains and on the boundless plains of Old Mexico and the American Southwest. His life has been cast along with these old stories, in the days when the old-timers lived and searched for gold. He has spent many pleasant hours around campfires listening to the tales and traditions of by-gone days.

Everyone dreams of finding buried riches. Many volumes of fiction have been written about the buried booty of the pirates who once sailed the seas. But this book is about treasure which is known to have existed, and which the old-timers insist will still be found. Here are the clues the writer has gathered in his years in the Desert Southwest. This is not a book of fiction. But those who hunt for these long lost fortunes should be cautious. They should heed the warning of whitened skulls, of lost trails and empty canteens.

And to each lost mine seeker — Good Luck!

JOHN D. MITCHELL

July 1, 1953

CONTENTS

ILLUSTRATIONS

PEGLEG'S BLACK NUGGETS

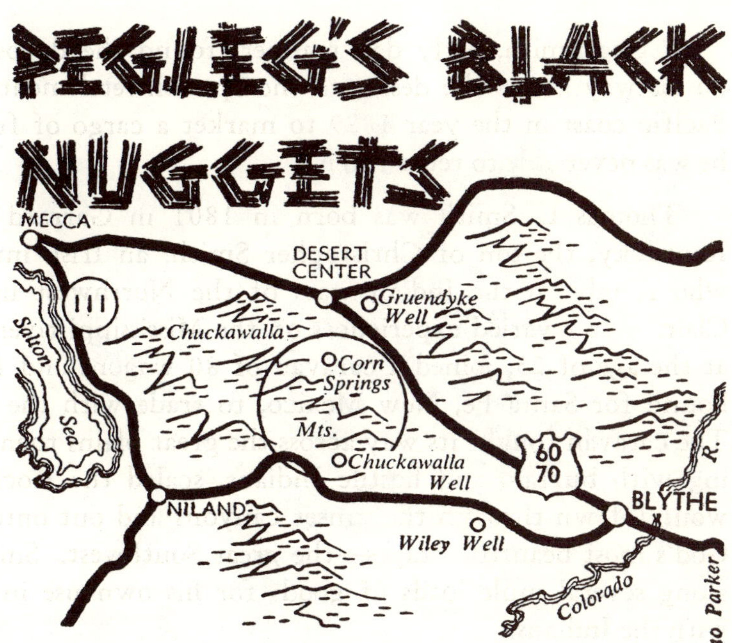

THE LOST PEGLEG SMITH gold mine with its piles of black gold nuggets is one of the celebrated traditions of the great Southwest. Much time and money have been spent and many lives lost in the quest for this fabulously rich gold deposit believed to be located in the heart of the great California desert—the Sahara of America.

For more than a century, prospectors and adventurers from every part of the civilized world have searched these wastelands for some trace of the "Lost Valley of the Phantom Buttes" from whence came the many black gold nuggets brought out of the desert by the Indians and the few white men who were willing to gamble their lives against those twin demons of the desert—heat and thirst.

Pegleg Smith, early day trapper, found the deposit while on his way across the desert to the Spanish settlements on the Pacific coast in the year 1829 to market a cargo of furs. But he was never able to return to it.

Thomas L. Smith was born in 1801 in Garrard county, Kentucky, the son of Christopher Smith, an Irish immigrant who fought in the Indian wars of the Northwest under St. Clair. After varied experiences on the Mississippi river, Smith, at the age of 23, joined a caravan of 80 wagons and 150 men bound for Santa Fe, New Mexico, to trade with the Indians. The caravan fought its way across the great plains then swarming with buffalo and hostile Indians, scaled the Rockies and wound down through the sunset canyons and out onto one of God's most beautiful stages—the great Southwest. Smith took along several mule loads of goods for his own use in trading with the Indians.

Shortly after arriving in Santa Fe, young Smith joined another large party bound for the Snake and Utah Indian territory. Later this party split up into smaller companies, and Smith and his men returned to the Grand river country in Colorado where they became involved with the Indians and Smith was shot in the leg while trying to bring in the body of a dead companion. The heavy arrow shattered the bone of his left leg just above the ankle. Smith borrowed a butcher knife from the camp cook and completed the job. After the wound had been bandaged, he was placed on a litter between two mules and carried 150 miles to a Snake Indian village where the squaws nursed him back to health.

When the stub leg had healed sufficiently to enable him to get around, Smith fashioned a wooden leg from an ash tree.

Henceforth he was known to his companions and the Indians as Pegleg.

Here amid snowcapped peaks, tumbling waterfalls, quiet lakes and swift running streams the little party hunted wild game, trapped beaver and lived the life of sturdy pioneers. Pegleg and his companions trapped the tributaries of the Virgin and the Colorado down to the junction of the Gila, arriving there in 1829.

Here, on the site of what later became the town of Yuma, Smith and another trapper named LaRue were intrusted with the task of taking a mule train of pelts to the Spanish settlements on the Pacific coast. Ahead of these men lay one of the most arid deserts in the American Southwest—the great Salton Sink.

It was into this no man's land that Pegleg and LaRue plunged with 15 or 20 pack animals loaded with furs and kegs of water. After floundering through the soft sand for days and making dry camps at night, it became increasingly apparent they would never be able to get out of the desert with their heavy loads of furs and the small amount of water they had left. It was decided to cache half of the furs in the sand dunes.

Late one evening Smith and LaRue camped at the base of the Chocolate mountains near three small black buttes. To get his bearings and if possible locate some green spot where water might be found, Smith climbed to the top of the highest butte. On his way down his attention was attracted by some black pebbles that lay scattered over the sides and around the base of the butte. Picking up several of them he found they were very heavy, and he put some of them in his pocket. Finally the men found their way out through a pass to the northwest, and at the foot of a green mountain they found cottonwood trees and a good supply of spring water.

Upon their arrival in the Spanish settlements on the coast, Smith was told that the black pebbles were solid gold which in some unknown manner had been coated over by nature with a thin film of manganese. After they had marketed their first load of furs they returned to the desert and brought out the balance, and with the proceeds of the combined sales they proceeded to go on a spree that lasted several weeks. After they had been ordered out of the settlement by the Spanish officials they rounded up a herd of horses and mules and headed for the Bear river country to the north.

In 1848, just before the stampede of the Argonauts, Pegleg was back again in the desert searching for the three black buttes where years before he had picked up the black nuggets. Finally he gave up the search and returned to San Francisco where he died in 1866.

During the 87 years which have intervened since the death of Pegleg Smith the story of his fabulous discovery—with many variations—has become a legend of the desert country. It became impossible to attribute to one man all the experiences told about Pegleg Smith, so a second Pegleg Smith has been conceived. Many of the old prospectors who have spent years looking for the black nuggets firmly believe there were two Peglegs—and that both of them actually found the lost butte of the gold nuggets.

There is still another legend bearing on the Pegleg discovery. The story is that in the middle of the last century a white man was guided to the gold by Indians, and he reported the three buttes were part of the rim of a great volcanic crater, and that he was almost overcome with gas fumes welling up from its floor. However, he and his Indian companion were able to bring out about 50 pounds of the black-coated metal, and eventually received $65,000 for their treasure.

My own connection with this strange adventure dates back about 25 years to the little town of Parker, Arizona, on the Colorado river. Some of the older inhabitants of the place had been telling me about a large meteor that had streaked through the night sky only a few years before. They said that the vacuum or suction created by it was so great that it had picked up empty oil barrels on the platform at the depot in the little town of Vidal, California, just across the river, and pulled them down the track for several thousand feet.

A great explosion was heard a few seconds later and it was believed to have struck a mountain a few miles south of Parker.

I was in the vicinity examining guano deposits at the time and decided to look for the meteorite. Later at Niland, California, I was informed by Mexicans that the meteorite had fallen northwest of that place and about 15 miles south of Corn springs. I returned to Blythe, California, and purchased a mule from a contractor who had the contract to grade the approaches to the Colorado river bridge. After purchasing a saddle, saddle bags and some provisions it became noised around town that I was headed for the Corn springs country and was told by some of the bootleggers that I had better stay away from Corn springs as it was headquarters for a tough bootlegger who would shoot on sight.

Next day I headed down the road through Palo Verde valley and made a dry camp the first night. The following morning I turned west along the old Bradshaw stage road and that night reached Chuckawalla well. I had just hobbled the mule and started supper on my little campfire when a young Mojave

Indian and his wife came into camp. He was mounted on an Indian pony and the girl was walking by his side carrying a small sack of jerky and pinole. They seemed grateful for the opportunity to share my evening meal and rest by the campfire. Like most Indians they were uncommunicative, and I did not press them for an answer as to where they were headed. Next morning after breakfast the woman filled the two-gallon canteen, hung it over the horn of the saddle and the man again mounted the horse and prepared to depart. I asked him why his wife did not ride and he replied, "Oh, she ain't got no horse." I watched them with some apprehension as they passed over the horizon and out of sight. It was the last time I ever saw them.

After prospecting for two days in the vicinity of the desert waterhole without finding any signs of the meteorite, I decided to head west to the road that runs from Mecca to Blythe. I left the next morning after an early breakfast, rode hard until about 5:00 o'clock in the afternoon. My water supply had dwindled to about one-half gallon, and the mule was showing signs of weariness. I had reached the eastern end of a long ridge or hogback.

Both the mule and I were tired and thirsty. While the blackened rocks and scorched earth in the immediate vicinity did not offer much hope, I felt that there must be water some place in the hills and sat down on a large rock to figure things out.

Presently I saw doves and other birds flying toward the south. I knew that birds flying rapidly in a straight line was a likely sign of water in that direction. I started to follow them and in a short time saw them break their flight in midair and drop down toward a break in the dark colored rocks.

A young Mojave came into camp riding a horse, his wife following behind on foot.

Further investigation disclosed a narrow crevice seven or eight feet wide and 50 or 60 feet long. A dolorite dike cut across the west end forming a natural tank in the hard bedrock, full of clear water. There was no broken pottery or any other signs in the vicinity that would indicate the tank was known to Indian or white man.

Not caring to disturb the birds that had unknowingly led me to their water supply, I made camp a short distance away.

After an early breakfast next morning, I filled my canteen, watered the mule and headed up the long ridge toward the western horizon. About 5:00 o'clock that afternoon I reached the summit and suddenly saw the top of a small black butte. As I rode forward, two smaller ones, one on each side, appeared. All three rose from a small valley or crater-like depression which was partly filled with white sand.

A brisk wind was blowing from the desert and a great yellow cloud came rolling up from the southeast. I knew that we were in for a sandstorm and hurriedly led the mule down into the crater and tied him to the limb of a dead ironwood tree that stood near a wall of rock. Hardly had I tied him and removed the saddle and bags of provisions and stored them under a shelving rock before the storm was upon us with all its force.

Sheets of fine sand poured over the edge of the crater like water over a waterfall. The swirling winds swept the bottom of the crater clean in places and piled the sand high in others. Not until about 4:00 o'clock in the morning did the wind cease to blow, and at daybreak I climbed out of the crater and cooked my breakfast.

Then, climbing the highest butte, I found it literally covered with black pebbles, nuggets of brown hematite and small boulders of white silica, all worn smooth. I picked up three of the stones and put them in my pocket. Later I gathered two small bags of them for I wanted to have them assayed.

I continued my search for the meteoric crater and at 3:00 o'clock the next afternoon found it. A 300-pound meteorite was partially buried in the gravel near the pit where the main mass had struck. I broke off a piece of it, and headed north through the Chuckawalla mountains toward the old Gruendyke well which I knew lay somewhere northwest of Corn springs. The going was hard, and to spare the mule I finally cached the two bags of rocks from the crater, planning to return for them later.

Late in the day I reached the Blythe-Mecca road and came upon a small covered wagon where a tall gray-haired man was cooking his supper of beans. He invited me to have a plate of them, with dutch oven biscuits. He said his name was John Anderson and he was trapping coyote and fox.

Twenty years later I met John Anderson in the Hell canyon country north of Prescott. He was very old, but he recalled our meeting in the Chuckawalla valley.

"Were you looking for the Lost Pegleg mine?" he asked.

I told him I had been out searching for a lost meteorite. This conversation recalled the three black stones I had picked up on that trip. Searching through my trunk later in the evening I found one of them. With a light tap of the hammer I broke off the black crust, and there was the loveliest gold nugget I have ever seen.

Someday I am going back to the Colorado desert, to search again for Pegleg's gold. If do not succeed in finding the "Lost Valley of the Phantom Buttes," I may at least find the $12,000 or $13,000 in black gold nuggets that I cached in the Chuckawalla mountains.

As I recall the black gold deposit, it is another of those rare chimneys that have always produced so much gold. I saw one from which a fortune in gold nuggets was taken. The Black Gold crater seems to be another chimney the top of which has been broken down by erosion, scattering the black gold nuggets, pieces of iron and small pebbles of white silica over the sides of the butte and around its base. Some chemical process in nature turned the nuggets black by coating them over with a film of manganese—"desert varnish," the old-timers call it.

With modern transportation I believe that one could make hurried trips in and out of the desert and bring out a large amount of gold from this deposit. Provided however, that he can locate the lost valley.

Most of the prospectors who have been looking for the Lost Pegleg have been searching too far south and have been following the lines of least resistance. It is located in the higher and more difficult part of the mountains and can be found by taking to the higher ridges and rough places and then only by accident. The buttes appear suddenly and cannot be seen from any direction until one is almost upon the edge of the crater.

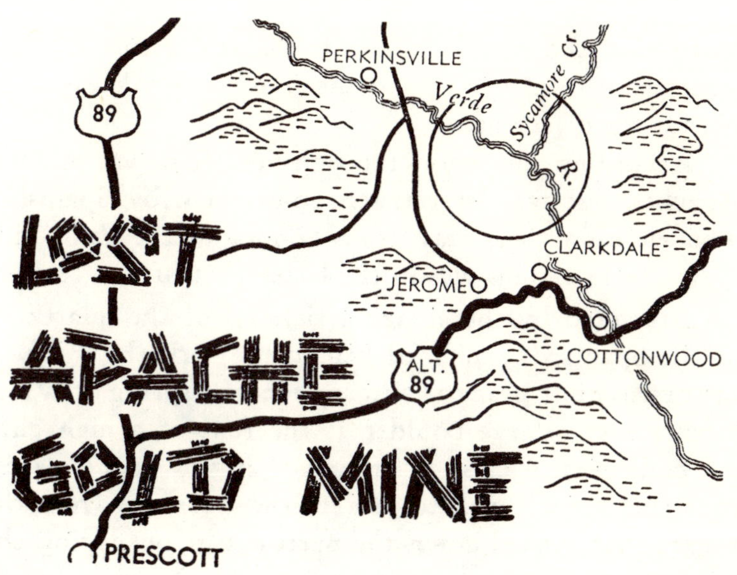

WHEN THE NOTORIOUS Apache outlaw Geronimo died in 1909 he carried with him to the happy hunting ground the secret of a rich gold mine that many white men would be glad to possess.

It is believed that certain Apaches still living know the approximate location of the mine, but since it is not on their reservation and it is unlikely they would profit from the disclosure, they prefer to remain silent.

After being captured in 1886, Geronimo used his knowledge of the gold mine in an effort to secure his release from Fort Sill, Oklahoma, where he was virtually a prisoner of the United States government. However, the plot was discovered before the wily old Indian with the aid of his conspirators could make his escape.

While Geronimo steadfastly refused to reveal the exact

location of the vein, he told a friend at the fort it was located somewhere in the wild and picturesque Verde river country, not far from Jerome.

According to rumor, the rich vein first was discovered by Apaches, but was later taken from them by Spanish soldiers who were on their way from Sonora to the Zuni villages in New Mexico. This was in the latter part of the 18th century.

Attracted by the amazing richness of the quartz vein, six of the Spaniards remained behind to work the mine. An arrastre was built near the outcrop where a spring of water broke from under a large boulder at the foot of a high cliff. The ore body was so close to an arroyo it was found necessary to construct a rock wall to protect the workings from the flood waters that rushed down the narrow canyon during the rainy season.

After a rock house had been constructed and the mining operations were well under way, a small adobe furnace was built and used to smelt the gold into heavy bars suitable for transportation by muleback.

The Apaches resented the intrusion of the Spaniards and lost no opportunity to harass them either by direct attack or by rolling large stones down on the workings from the high canyon walls.

The adventurers were heavily armed and were forced to fight as well as mine, but the ore was so rich they were reluctant to leave it. As the tunnel penetrated farther into the mountain the ore increased in richness until it was almost half gold and was taken directly to the smelter instead of the arrastre.

When operations had been carried on for a year or more and a large number of gold bars had been run and stored away in the tunnel, it was decided to load the gold on the backs of pack mules and return to Mexico for reinforcements in order to work the mine with more safety.

In their hurry to get away the Spaniards neglected to guard the narrow entrance to the canyon in which the mine was located, and as a result of this neglect they were attacked by a party of Apache warriors. In the fight that ensued many Apaches were either killed or wounded by the Spaniards who retreated to the rock wall and nearby house. However, four out of the six Spaniards were so badly wounded they died shortly after the Indians withdrew to the surrounding hills.

The two surviving Spaniards decided to hide the gold in the tunnel and make their escape as best they could. After burying their dead they mounted two saddle mules that had not been stolen by the Indians and under cover of darkness headed south. Ten days later the two Spaniards arrived at Tubac on the Santa Cruz river.

It was then 1767, and King Charles III had just issued his edict that expelled the Jesuits from Spain and all its possessions. As a result, the mines were closed and the missions were abandoned and either were destroyed by the Indians or fell into ruin from neglect.

The two old miners eventually made their way back to Mexico, but were never able to return to work the mine or recover the buried gold. They did, however, leave a map of the country in which the mine was located and a record of their operations.

Legendary lost mines are invariably richest where the Indians are wildest—and this one is no exception. Like most lost mine stories there are several versions and many "true" maps. In this case the most likely story is the one coming from the city of Mexico, which places the mine in the Sycamore canyon country between Jerome and Perkinsville, Yavapai county, Arizona. There are numerous small side canyons that empty their flood waters into the Sycamore and at least one of them answers the description set forth in the old document.

The old map shows the profile of an Indian's head sculptured by nature on a high cliff just above the mine opening. The nose of this rock Indian is very large and, as the story goes, the mine is located directly under the Indian's nose.

It is said there is such a cliff overlooking a narrow box canyon up in that part of the country, and the foundations of an old adobe or rock house are still visible. The rock fence or wall at the foot of the high cliff which was known to many old-time cowmen who ranged their cattle in that part of the country is now almost completely covered by a slide of rock broken from the canyon wall above.

A stream of water breaks under a large boulder near the canyon wall, and the ruins of an old *vaso* (adobe smelter) and the grinding stones of an arrastre may still be seen there. Not far away under the trees are several old graves all marked by piles of stone.

The deer and the bear, the wild picturesque canyon and the small stream of water are there. Also a deposit of rose quartz. But the golden treasure has never been rediscovered, if in fact it ever existed.

DON JOAQUIN AND HIS GOLD MINE

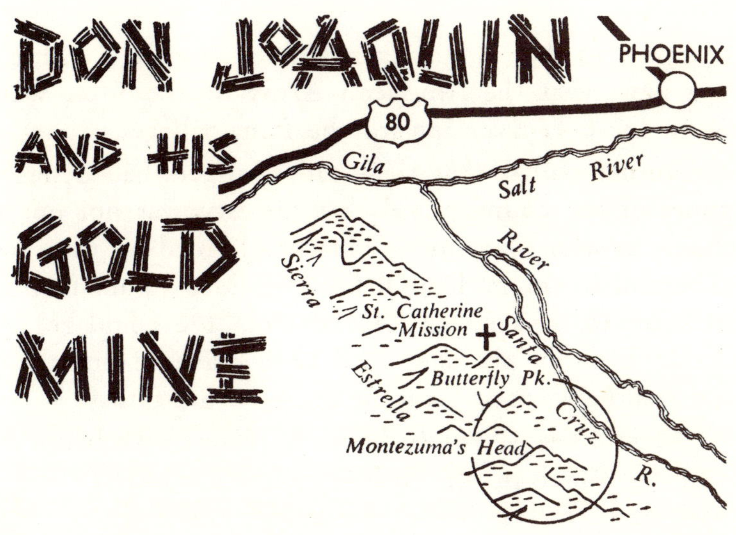

DEEP IN THE HEART of the Estrella mountains, south of Phoenix, Arizona, stand the tumble-down ruins of an old rock house. The walls are several feet thick and the loopholes around the top are mute evidence of the purpose for which the house was built—to protect the occupants against Apache Indians. In the bottom of the wild rocky canyon nearby are the partly caved workings of an ancient gold mine.

There is a tradition among the Pima and Maricopa Indians now living in the vicinity of the St. Catherine mission on the east side of the mountains, that their ancestors worked in the mine and that it belonged to an old Spaniard by the name of Don Joaquin Campoy, from Guadalajara, Mexico, and that he left a great treasure buried in a nearby cave.

According to the stories told by these Indians, the mine had been worked for a number of years when, in 1847, Indian scouts raced their ponies from village to village with the startling news that the American Army of the West was headed down the Gila river toward the Pima villages.

Rumor had it that these tall strangers had designs on the mines of the country and that honesty was not one of their characteristics. Becoming greatly alarmed at these wild and unfounded rumors, Don Joaquin decided to abandon his mine and flee to his beloved Guadalajara. He could return north again when the strangers had been driven from the country and resume work at his mine in peace and safety.

After a sleepless night he made plans to discharge the crew, start the Mexicans on their way to Guadalajara and the Indians back to their homes in the valley, then bury the treasure in some secret place in the mountains until he could return in safety for it.

In his possession were 50 bars of gold recovered from the ore taken from the vein, and 30 bags of gold nuggets from the placer operations in the canyon below where the rich vein outcropped. Who among his villainous crew of miners could be trusted to help him bury the gold and where should he hide it?

When the crew had been sent on their way, Don Joaquin chose an old Maricopa to help him load the 3,000 pounds of gold on the backs of 15 mules. When the last pack was in place and all was in readiness, the mules were headed up the steep trail toward Butterfly peak where they hoped to strike another trail leading down the high ridge past Montezuma's Head, which is near the south end of the range.

Late in the afternoon the pack mules, groaning under their loads of gold, came to a halt on the summit, and as the sound of the tinkling bell on the lead mule died away, the

Late in the afternoon the pack mules, groaning under their loads of gold, came to a halt on the summit, and as the sound of the tinkling bell on the lead mule died away, the two men sat down to rest.

two men sat down to rest. Far below them to the west at the bottom of the deep box canyon, at the end of a zig-zag trail, lay the old rock house and the mine workings. Below them to the east lay the green valley crossed by the Salt, Gila and Santa Cruz rivers that shown like silver threads in the setting sun. Far beyond the valley to the northeast the hoary heads of the Four Peaks stood silent guard over the upland plains.

The little pack train made its way slowly down the winding trail toward Montezuma's Head and when about half way down turned off the trail to the west and entered a short box canyon. They presently came to a halt in front of a cave. After the treasure had been unloaded and packed into the cave, the old Indian silently dug a deep hole in the soft dirt and guano that had accumulated near the back end.

The sun had long since gone down behind the ragged edge of the western world and the canyon lay dark and shadowy ahead. This was to be the last resting place of the treasure. The hole completed, the heavy bars were dropped in first and then the leather bags of placer gold. When the last bag dropped with a thud the old Maricopa fell forward into the hole on top of the gold—struck dead by a club in the hands of Don Joaquin.

Hurriedly filling the hole with bat guano and dirt, the old man paused to view his work with grim satisfaction, and then, after marking the spot on a map that he carried with him, headed the pack train down the trail past Montezuma's Head and out onto the flat country at the south end of the range.

Don Joaquin overtook the miners at the little butte that stands in the valley only a short distance southeast of the Estrellas where they had gone into camp for the night. As they sat around the campfire a feeling of confidence unmingled with remorse seemed to comfort the old man.

At sunrise the next morning Don Joaquin was found dead in his blankets. The body was laid to rest at the foot of the little butte and marked with a cairn of stones that may be seen there today.

Pima and Maricopa Indians claim that the map fell into the hands of one of the Mexican miners upon the death of Don Joaquin and that about 30 years after the signing of the Gadsden Treaty, this Mexican miner, then an old man, came north with the map in an effort to relocate the mine and treasure. Owing to the fact that the Apache Indians were then on the warpath and the Maricopas and Pimas refused to lead him to it, he returned to Mexico without accomplishing his purpose.

Many people including the writer have seen the old rock house and the mine workings in the canyon below it. The vein is a true fissure cutting gneiss with a strike north 30° and east and dips 40° to the southeast. Some free gold was observed in the 18-inch vein at the top of the shaft. From all indications on the spot work must have been carried on over a long period of time both in the shaft and open cuts and in the placer operations in the canyon below the mine.

It is believed that some of the older Indians know the location of the cave, but because one of their tribesmen was killed there, refuse to go near it or direct anyone else to it. However, they say that two young Indians, riding after cattle many years ago in the wild lands around the southern tip of the Estrellas, suddenly were overtaken by a storm and were forced to seek shelter in a nearby cave. The storm raged on and the wind howled down through the hills from the north.

The two cowboys decided to spend the night in the cave to protect themselves from the cold. About midnight the storm abated and they were startled by a rustling noise just outside the entrance and by a weird white light that suddenly appeared from the floor near the back of the cave. The noise outside ceased and the light disappeared as suddenly as it had come.

The Army of the West, after trading with the friendly Pimas, passed down the valley and over the hills. Don Joaquin in his lonely grave by the little butte sleeps on. The mine in the deep canyon at the end of the zig-zag trail is still unworked and the treasure lies undisturbed in the cave.

Montezuma's Treasure

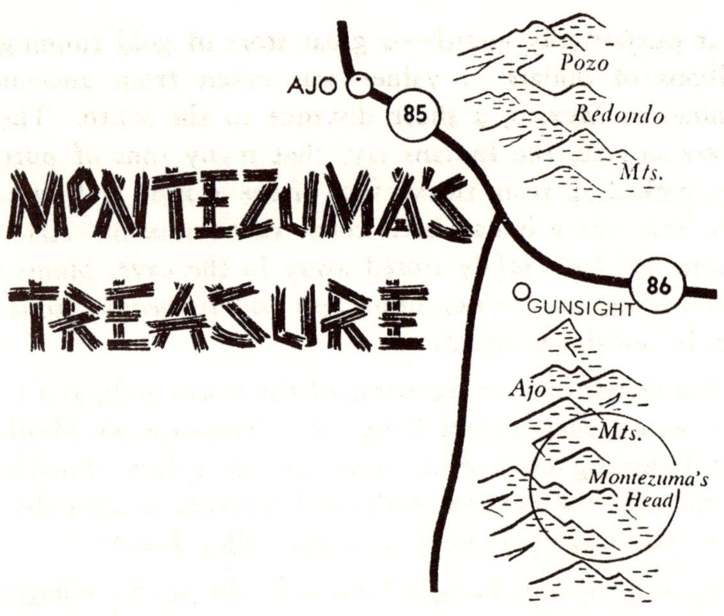

IT WAS IN THE little mining town of Ajo, Pima County, Arizona, that I first heard the story of Montezuma's treasure. Hidden away for more than four centuries in the secret recesses of the barren and fantastic Ajo mountains below Montezuma's Head, the legend relates, is a treasure hoard of such wonderful riches that it has been watched constantly for 300 years, and to this day no Indian will disclose its location. The Papagos say that their ancestors helped bury the treasure in a mountain cave beneath the stony landmark, and that it is guarded by none other than Montezuma himself.

For a hundred miles in every direction from the Ajo mountains this lofty peak resembling the head and shoulders of an Indian can be seen clearly outlined against the sky. The treasure it purportedly guards—a great store of gold running into millions of dollars in value—was taken from ancient placer mines in Mexico, a short distance to the south. The mines were so rich, the Indians say, that many tons of pure gold were picked up from the surface of the ground and from the creek beds where it had been collected by erosion. After the treasure had been safely stored away in the cave, Montezuma climbed up to the mountain top and turned to stone. And there he remains to this day.

The Ajo mountains are the home of the storm gods, and in the rainy season dark clouds hang over Montezuma's Head, flashes of lightning chase each other up the ridges, thunder rumbles through the canyon walls, and torrents of rain descend from the mountain sides into the valley below.

During such storms, Papago Indians in the nearby villages sit around the campfires and in hushed tones talk about the great treasure stored away in the mountain cave. They believe that some day the spirit of Montezuma will come out of the east. He will climb down from the mountain top and open the secret cave, and all its wealth will be given to the Indians to whom it rightfully belongs.

Of the many thousand travelers who pass over the highway between Tucson and Ajo each year, few have heard the legend of the wealth stored away in the sombre mountain beneath Montezuma's Head. Those who have heard the story and who would search for the treasure have one clue to the cave's location: "When the Indians were engaged in storing the gold in the cave," relates an old Papago legend, "they were so close that, on a still night, they could hear the tom-toms beat and the dogs bark in the village below."

MANY YEARS HAVE PASSED since the sweet-toned bells of Guevavi rang out over upland plains and verdant valleys, calling Indian neophytes to early morning prayer. The quaint old mission dates back to the year 1691.

This Jesuit mission is near the little farming community of Calabasas, a short distance northeast of Nogales, Arizona. While the Hispano-Americans in that region have always regarded it as an agricultural mission, there are rumors that this was not always true. The padres, needing metal with which to mold bells, church service and household utensils and other articles, are said to have sent out Indian miners to search the surrounding hills for suitable ores.

From among the specimens brought in, the Spanish fathers chose the heavy black silver-copper ore which is believed to have come from the head of a rocky canyon in the southwest end of rugged San Cayetano mountain a short distance north of the mission. When the bells were molded the padres and their Indian helpers were so pleased with the beautiful church and its belfry bells it was at once decided to continue to work the mine. Accordingly the ore was mined and carried on the backs of mules to the furnace which had been constructed near the mission. After the altar had been supplied with beautiful hand-molded candlesticks and other articles, the padres turned their attention to the fashioning of cups, plates, bowls and other utensils of table and household use made from the *planchas de plata* recovered from the smelting of the rich ore brought down daily from the mine.

The mine was said to be so close to the mission the miners could hear the sweet-toned bells ringing in the little pueblo on the east bank of the wide arroyo. After all the needs of the church and the padres' quarters had been supplied, the bullion was run into heavy bars and stored in a secret place for future shipment to Spain, or for sale in the City of Mexico. One fifth of all bullion from the many rich mines worked by the Jesuits belonged to the King of Spain and was known as the Royal Fifth. Failure on the part of the Jesuits to pay this royal tax is said to have been one of the reasons why King Charles III issued an edict expelling all Jesuits from Spain and its possessions.

In 1751 occurred the second revolt of the Pima tribes, in which the padres at Caborca and Sonoyta were murdered and the beautiful missions of San Xavier and Guevavi were plundered and partly destroyed. Then, in 1767 the expulsion edict was issued, and the Jesuits, unable to take anything with them, sealed the entrances to the mines, buried their treasures and fled to the coast. Many of them were killed by hostile Indians before they reached ships that were to return them to Spain.

At Guevavi, according to legend, the bells, altar service, candlesticks, household and cooking utensils were all collected and stored in a secret hiding place near the mission ruins, where they have remained to this day.

The first Americans to arrive in Santa Cruz valley in 1859 found large piles of slag at Tubac, Tumacacori, Cerro Colorado and Guevavi. Most of the slag was rich in silver and was shipped at a good profit by the miners who discovered it. At Guevavi most of the land on which the old adobe smelter and slag pile stood has been cultivated and there remain no signs of the old furnace. However, rich pieces of silver ore are now and then turned up by the plow.

For many years Juan Bustamante, an old woodchopper and pocket miner, lived with his son-in-law and only daughter in a shack in the shade of spreading cottonwoods that line the east bank of the wide arroyo near the mission ruins. Old Juan made his living in the hot summer months by panning the gulches for fine gold and by peddling wood in Nogales during the winter months when the ground was too wet for dry washing operations. Juan was well-known at the assay office of old Charley Taylor and among merchants and residents here he sold his small vials of placer gold and peddled his burro loads of stove wood.

One hot summer day about 35 years ago old Juan arrived at Taylor's assay office with his two burros loaded down with sacks of rich silver ore, instead of the usual cargo of stove wood and small vial of placer gold. This caused considerable excitement among the miners who hung out at the assay office, but no amount of coaxing by Taylor or the American miners would induce the wily old Indian to disclose the source of his newly

One day old Juan arrived at the assay office with his two burros loaded down with rich silver ore.

found wealth. Taylor said the ore was the richest that he had seen in many years. It had small pieces of grey quartz adhering to it and showed evidence of having come from the mineral district to the north of Nogales, around old Tumacacori mission or Cerro Colorado which has long been noted for its rich silver bearing veins.

Old Juan was fond of but two things. He loved to smoke innumerable cigarettes rolled in corn husks, and he liked to drink the red wine which he called *Sangre de Cristo.* There is a superstition among many of the old-time Spanish-Americans that if they will bathe in running water on San Juan day, June 24, it will insure good health for the coming year. So it came about that every year after taking his annual bath in a nearby arroyo, old Juan loaded his faithful jacks with rich silver-copper ore and wandered south to El Pueblo de Nogales, for the fiesta of San Juan. On the second day of the great fiesta, Juan, full of his beloved Sangre de Cristo, frijolitas, tacos and tortillas, lay down on his serape for a little siesta. In his troubled sleep, the old *gambucino* talked loud and long about a rich silver mine he had discovered high up in a rocky canyon on the southwest side of the rugged San Cayetano mountains. A newly made friend, not quite so drunk, listened in on old Juan's conversation and the day after fiesta set out with a companion to search for the mine.

After several days of hard work, the two Mexicans found some very heavy silver-copper ore at the mouth of the deep rocky canyon described by Juan in his troubled sleep. High up near the head of the canyon they came upon a partly burned crucifix that had evidently been washed from the tunnel. It has long been a custom among Mexican and Indian miners to place a crucifix in the mouth of any mine in which they are working. The crucifix was taken to the Tumacacori mission where it remained for many years. The two men made many trips to the locality but were unable to find any trace of the rich vein or the old tunnel. The heavy rains that annually fall in that locality had evidently covered it over.

Old Juan made several secret trips to the mine after the fiesta. Juan's last load of ore was purchased by Taylor for $150. The next day he arrived at the little house of his son-in-law with his two burros loaded down with provisions and a supply of red wine. He was found dead on his pallet the next morning. Neither the mine nor the great treasure buried near the mission walls has ever been found.

BURIED TREASURE OF DON FELIPE

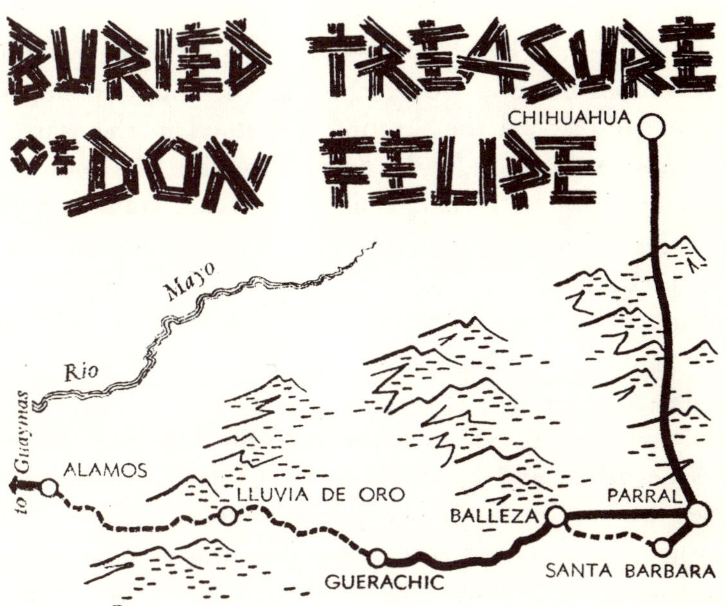

IN THE QUAINT OLD TOWN of Alamos, Sonora, Mexico, lived a wealthy Spaniard, Don Felipe. His land stretched over a vast area covering Rancho Santa Barbara at the base of Guadalupe mountain in the foothills of the Sierra Madre range. The Mayo river rushes down through the narrow gorges past Guadalupe, then makes a great bend around a high point of land that juts out to the north and on which stands the old ranch house like a feudal castle, vividly outlined against the sky. From here the river flows gently through the peaceful Mayo valley and out to the Gulf of California.

My first view of Santa Barbara was from the top of Guadalupe mountain. From the early morning until nearly noon the saddle mules toiled up the steep trail that leads to the summit from the valley below. A light rain was falling and the clouds hung low over the rugged mountain slopes. About noon we reached the summit and stood in the warm sunlight far above the clouds. In every direction the mountain peaks stood out above the clouds like beautiful islands in a silvery sea.

The clouds parted and there nestling at our feet was old Santa Barbara, covered with roses and bougainvillea and surrounded by orange groves and green fields of growing grain.

Santa Barbara dates back to the time of the Spanish Conquistadores, and was originally owned by Don Felipe, whose only interest in life was the hoarding of gold and silver for his beautiful and only daughter, Clotilde, whose mother had died at her birth. Many peons were employed in the fields to grow and harvest the grain that was needed to supply the wants of the Indians who worked in the great silver mine on Guadalupe mountain and in the gold mines at Sobia, just over the mountains to the west.

Two or three times a week large numbers of pack mules loaded with gold and silver bars would come down to Santa Barbara from the mines. The tinkling bells on the lead mules could be heard a long way off, and Don Felipe often rode out on his mule to meet them. Upon arrival at Santa Barbara, the mules always were taken inside through a large arched doorway and the precious cargo unloaded. The mules were then loaded with corn and flour and other supplies needed at the mines.

Twice each year a pack train was sent to Mexico City, with one-fifth of all the bullion that had been produced from the mines of Don Felipe. This belonged to the King of Spain, and was known as the Royal Fifth. The years passed, and Don Felipe profited greatly from his agricultural and mining operations. Clotilde, who spent much time at the ranch, grew more beautiful as she developed into young womanhood. Three times each week the band played music soft and low, and Clotilde, accompanied by Dona Maria, her *duena,* strolled among the flowers on the plaza in front of the little white chapel where she often went to pray.

When the revolution broke out in 1810, Santa Barbara was attacked by Indians and Don Felipe was killed by an arrow shot from the bow of a Yaqui warrior. Upon seeing her father fall, Clotilde rushed to his side and was about to be captured, when she suddenly drew from under her mantilla a large picture of the Saint Guadalupe, which she held before her. When the Indians saw their patron saint, they fled in great disorder. Dona Maria took Clotilde to Mexico City and placed her in a convent to be educated. Many years later the search for the mines and great treasure began.

No one knew where Don Felipe hid the bullion after it had been unloaded in the patio. The gold mines at Sobia were relocated and produced a large amount of gold. The Guadalupe silver mine has never been found. It was sealed up with all the tools inside. Rumor has it that the treasure was buried in an underground room inside the walls, and that every year a strange light appears in that vicinity.

The Mayo Indians believe that there is something about buried gold and silver that causes it to glow in warm weather when the ground is wet. So every year when the warm June rains begin, they look for the strange lights to appear.

One dark night when a light rain was falling, one of the great spotted jaguars or Mexican tigers that inhabit caves in the nearby Moche Cowie mountains, entered the house of an Indian through an open door and carried off a three-year-old child who was asleep on a pallet near the door. The frantic cries of the mother aroused the village, but the great beast had already carried the child into the thick underbrush.

Just as the Mayos were running to notify the padre at the church, the strange light appeared again inside the walls. All the buildings could be seen plainly in the weird, white, shimmering light.

Every year in June when the rains come, the light appears and the search for the great treasure goes on. But it never has been found. Don Felipe's bullion still lies hidden in the secret treasure vault somewhere in the peaceful Mayo valley.

LOST JOHN CLARK SILVER MINE

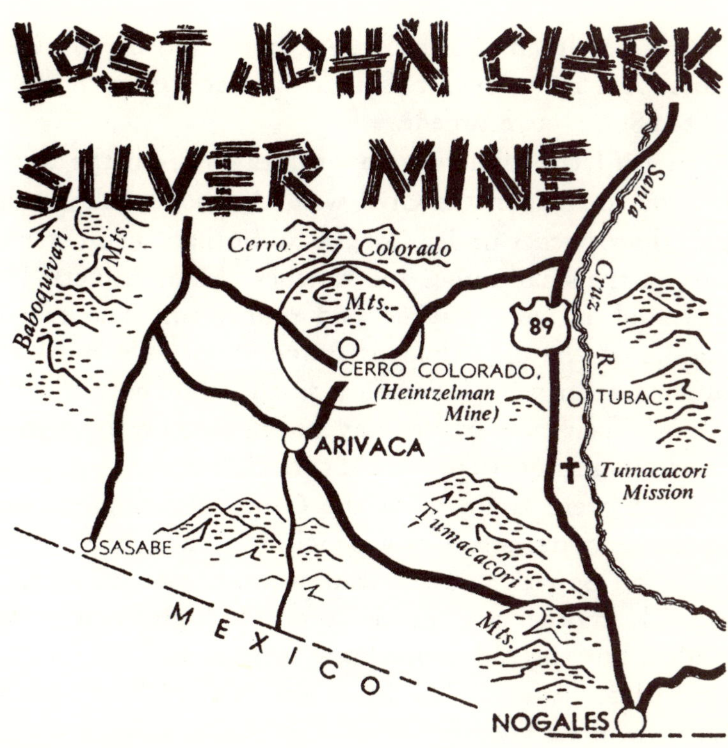

SOMEWHERE IN THE Cerro Colorado mining district, southern Pima county, Arizona, is an old mine shaft believed to be about 125 feet deep and to contain, besides a rich silver vein, 40 tons of silver ore assaying 2000 ounces to the ton. The mine was discovered and worked for a short time by a man named John Clark, who left St. Louis, Missouri, in the early '50s to prospect for gold and silver in the mountains of the West. Making his way across plains swarming with hostile Indians, he came finally to the Cerro Colorado district where he located a vein of rich silver ore.

The Heintzelman, Austerlitz, Albatross and many other noted mines were being operated under protection furnished by the United States government.

In 1861 the soldiers were withdrawn from the territory of Arizona to fight in the Civil war. As soon as the troops were gone the Apaches under Cochise and others again started their raids on the small mines and ranches. Many miners, freighters and ranchers were waylaid and murdered. The two original locators of the old Albatross mine about five miles south of Cumaro wash were killed in a small cabin near the mine entrance. Their twin graves may still be seen on the high bank of the arroyo just north of the old tunnel.

Raids were frequent at the Canoa and Sopori ranches on the Santa Cruz, and many people lost their lives. During an attack on Sopori an American woman gave birth to a baby girl. The mother was murdered on the high point of rock just across from the old adobe ruins where she along with others had fled for safety. The baby was rescued later and grew to womanhood in Tucson.

Two Mexican bandits, disguised as miners, secured work at the Heintzelman mine and a few days later, when they had familiarized themselves with the lay of the land, murdered John Poston, the superintendent, and eleven other employes. The Mexican miners joined the bandits in looting the mine offices, store and the ore bins at the mine. In their haste to reach the border ahead of the officers they were forced to abandon much of the stolen loot. The road from the mine to Saric, Sonora, was strewn with merchandise taken from the store.

When the officers arrived from Tucson several days later they found the bodies of John Poston and eleven employes,

The early day miners had to fight as well as mine.

both men and women, scattered over the hillside between the store and the mine. The bodies of the dead were buried on the little red hill just north of the old store and office buildings, only the foundations of which now remain. The foundation of a round watch tower at the northwest corner would seem to indicate that the early day miners had to fight as well as mine.

Clark packed his ore in strong leather bags and had made one shipment of 40 tons to St. Louis, with a caravan from the Heintzelman mine. This shipment netted him $80,000, as silver at that time was worth $1.00 per ounce. When the soldiers were withdrawn and the Apaches again started their raids, Clark had 40 tons mined and stored in a small rock house near the shaft. Foreseeing that he would be unable to ship this ore with any certainty of it reaching its destination, he threw it back in the ground and pulled the timbers out around the collar of the shaft, allowing the loose dirt to cave in on the ore and the vein from which it had been mined.

Clark and the other miners and ranchers who had not been

killed abandoned their mines and ranches and fled to Tucson for safety. The Apaches continued their raids until 1886, when by the joint operations of the American and Mexican governments they were rounded up and placed on reservations where they have remained to this day.

Clark died in the east, silver was demonetized and the old mines, with few exceptions, have lain idle ever since. All records of Clark's early day operations seem to have been lost. The late Mrs. Mary Black, wife of Judge Black, pioneer jurist of Santa Cruz county, taught school at the Heitzelman mine in the early '60s and knew Clark well. She told the writer she saw the pile of rich ore that Clark threw back in the old shaft. She further stated that the shaft was located some distance from the Heintzelman mine and that it was on one of the great fault fissures along which the rich ore bodies of the district are found. These fissures are in the old andesite and are water courses through which the rich mineralized solutions circulate. Wherever a vein or hard dike cuts across the fault it has a tendency to dam up the solutions causing them to precipitate the rich ore in great bodies of highgrade silver-copper. The rain water that falls on these soft outcrops forms a weak solution of sulfuric acid which leaches the silver-copper and carries it down to water level where it is precipitated as secondary enrichment. The soft outcrops are made up of kaolin and iron stained quartz badly crushed. Occasionally rich pieces of ore that have resisted the leaching process are washed out by heavy rains.

In the early days the Mexican miners would leave their work after each storm to hurry along these fault fissures and gather up these rich pieces of float, which often assayed from 5000 to 6000 ounces silver and 25 per cent copper. One good chunk was often enough to buy sowbelly and beans for several months.

Clark's mine was somewhat isolated, and it was not unusual to see small bands of Apache warriors riding the high ridges just out of shooting distance for the old-time rifles in use by the soldiers and miners throughout the country. A sub-chief called Bobtailed Coyote and known to the American and Mexican miners as Robert T. Wolf, passed Clark's camp frequently. One day, when about half drunk, he left his little band of warriors out on the flats and came into camp alone. He was in a surly mood and demanded ammunition, tobacco, grub and more firewater, threatening to raid the camp if he did not get it. Clark told him that while he was short on all the above named articles, he did have some strong medicine with which he could lick hell out of the chief and any number of his warriors.

Clark was bothered with rheumatism and on one of his trips east he had purchased one of those old time electric machines used throughout the east by quack doctors. Clark had set the machine up in the back room of his cabin and had been having a lot of fun trying it out on the Mexican miners and freighters in the camp. Naturally the drunken Indian was anxious to know more about the white man's strong medicine. After some persuasion the Indian took hold of the handles which had been run through the wall into the front room. At a given signal one of Clark's friends in the back room turned on the juice by cranking the machine. The chief got the surprise of his life, and when the cranking stopped and he was able to turn loose the handles he rushed out the front door and never stopped running until he had reached the little band of warriors he had left on the flats.

Bobtailed Coyote continued to ride the high ridges just out of rifle range, but never again came into camp. However, always when passing that way he never failed to dismount and walk up to the top of a little hill and go through some insulting movements. This annoyed Clark and he decided to teach him a lesson that he would not soon forget.

One of Clark's friends in the East had sent him a high-powered rifle that had just been put on the market. This gun carried several yards farther than the guns then in use in the West.

Sometime later the chief and his band of warriors were seen riding the high ridge just east of the mine. As had been his custom in the past, Bobtailed Coyote dismounted, climbed to the top of the little hill on the prairie and prepared to start his show. Clark poked the barrel of his rifle through a crack in the wall and waited. When the chief was humped over Clark fired, putting a bullet through the fat part of his buttock. The chief jumped about six feet into the air and let out a lusty war-whoop. He hit the ground running and the last seen of Bobtailed Coyote he was going over a hump in the prairie as fast as any buck Indian had ever done before or since.

Since the Apaches were rounded up in 1886, Mexican and Indian *gambucinos* have made a good living working these old silver mine dumps. There is not much left on the surface, but any prospector or miner able to read the surface indications should be able to find something good in these old silver mining camps that have so long been idle. Then too, there always remains the possibility of running onto the old Clark shaft with the 40 tons of 2000-ounce silver ore at the bottom.

LOST PICK MINE

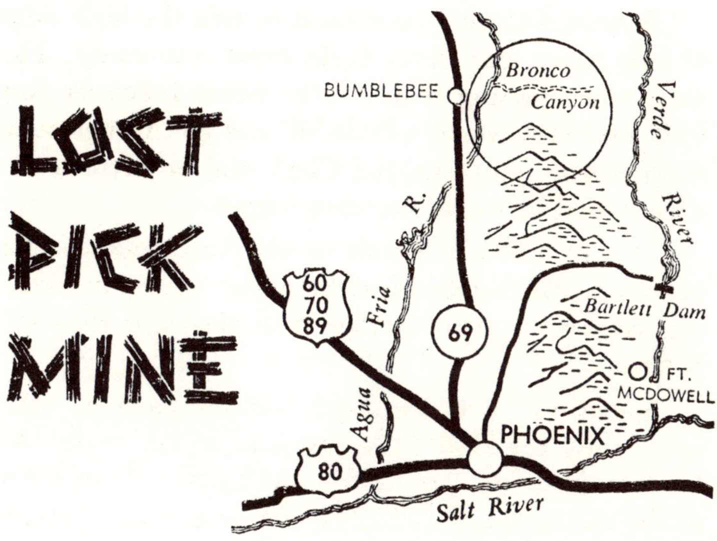

IT WAS RUMORED in the frontier town of Phoenix in 1871, that an old Apache Indian was bartering rich chunks of gold ore for supplies at the store in Fort McDowell. The Apache was known to live up in the Bronco canyon country about 50 miles north of Phoenix and 25 miles northwest of the fort.

The bartering had been going on for about a year when two prospectors by the name of Brown and Davis came into the country from Phoenix. They happened to be in the store one day when the old Apache came in with his pockets full of the rich ore which was matted together with coarse wires and nuggets of gold. The two prospectors were old-timers, but in all their experience they had never seen such rich rock.

Having bartered his gold, the Indian started off across the desert. After traveling about 10 miles he dropped down into

Coon creek canyon and followed that up to where it joins the east fork of Bronco canyon.

There the trail was lost by the two prospectors who had been following a few miles behind the Indian.

Returning to the fort the two men purchased supplies sufficient to last them several weeks and then headed their burros out across the desert in the direction of Wild Bronco canyon. That night they camped at a small spring on the south fork of the canyon where a stream of water bubbled from the west bank and ran several hundred feet before losing itself in the sand.

One day while prospecting in the wild brush covered country on the west side of the canyon they discovered an 18-inch quartz vein very rich in free gold similar in form to that they had seen in the hands of the Indian. The vein outcropped in a patch of manzanita brush and showed every evidence of having been worked. Little piles of ore were scattered along the vein and under the palo verde trees that grew nearby. Pottery sherds strewn over the ground indicated that the vein had been worked by Indian squaws.

Brown and Davis returned to their camp at the spring and constructed a crude arrastre in which to grind the rich ore. After 25 sacks of the quartz had been mined and milled, the partners estimated they had in the neighborhood of $70,000 or $80,000 in gold in their possession. Their pannings indicated that the ore would assay around $80,000 per ton in gold. As fast as the amalgam was taken from the floor of the arrastre it was rolled into balls and stored in a hole under a large rock that stood near the arrastre on the east bank of the creek.

With all this wealth the partners decided to return to their old home in San Francisco, where after a few months' rest they would purchase machinery and return to work their mine.

Early in the morning as they were getting ready to break camp, a small party of Apache warriors emerged from the rocks near the arrastre and started firing. Davis, the younger of the two prospectors, fell dead with a bullet through his head. Brown grabbed his rifle and sprang behind a large boulder as six Apaches made a rush for the camp. From his place of concealment Brown killed three of the Apaches and wounded a fourth. The others abandoned the fight and disappeared into the rocky canyon.

Brown crawled into the manzanita thicket and escaped with his rifle and the clothes he had on his back. A piece of rich ore he carried in his pocket was assayed in San Francisco some years later and was found to contain $84,000 a ton in gold.

Brown kept his secret, awaiting the time when it would be safe to return to the Indian country.

Eventually the Indians were pacified and placed on reservations. Then, although he was now 80 years of age, the prospector decided to return to the scene of the strike.

He reached Phoenix on his way to the Bronco canyon country, but while he was gathering supplies and an outfit to accompany him into the desert wilderness, he was taken ill and placed in a hospital.

On his deathbed he told for the first time the story of the strike he and Davis had made, and of the fight with the Indians. The balls of amalgam, he said, were buried in a shallow hole between a large boulder and a stratum of white volcanic ash that outcrops along the foot of the mountains on the east side of the little valley. The gold probably was still there, unless the Apaches had seen it buried and had taken it.

Several years later a Mexican goat-herder in that area came across the site of an old mining camp, and reported that he had seen a rusty pick sticking in a crevice in a small quartz vein, but did not stop to investigate. This story tallied closely with Brown's dying statement that his partner's pick was in the quartz when he was killed by the Indians. The Mexican had disappeared, however, before the story of the pick reached those who knew about the lost gold mine.

It is said that a circle of rocks indicating the location of an ancient arrastre may be found in that region today, but neither the pick nor the cache of gold has been relocated as far as is known.

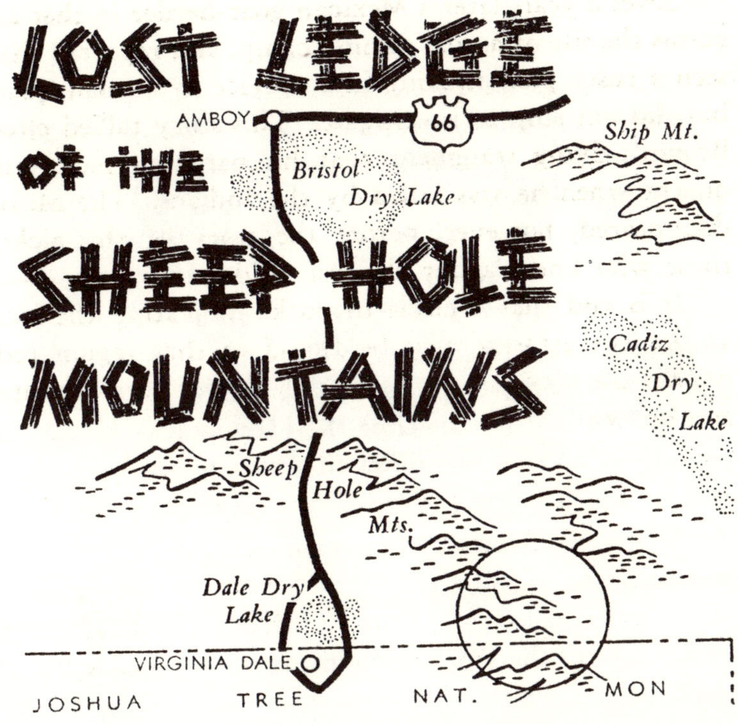

MOST LOST MINE STORIES leave the reader with the impression that the richest mines were found and lost in wild Indian country by old prospectors with long whiskers—the wilder the Indians and the longer the prospector's or desert rat's whiskers, the richer the mine. The Lost Ledge of the Sheep Hole mountains fills half of this lost mine tale "recipe." The old prospector had plenty of whiskers, but there were no wild Indians.

Early one summer morning about 50 years ago old Pete Ring; John Lock, storekeeper; Jim Walsh, section foreman;

Bill Pine, Santa Fe station agent, and the writer were standing on the depot platform at Amboy, California. A number of strange objects were seen bobbing up and down on top of the heat waves that hung over the dry lake southeast of the station. The lake bed had filled with clear water, and the dancing heat waves had lifted everything high into the warm air above the ground. Even old Pete Ring's mine that stood on a small brown hill near the eastern edge of the lake seemed to be high up in the clouds with fairy palaces all around it. As we stood looking at the strange objects dancing around in the shimmering mirage, Pete Ring remarked, "Hell, that's Hermit John and his outfit." By the time the Hermit had reached the western edge of the mirage his outfit was down on the ground again, and he was heading for the Santa Fe depot.

While the Hermit was very secretive about his business, he was by no means a total stranger to the few residents of the little desert railroad station. This was the third time he had shown up at the store and railroad station. Despite the fact that the tall white whiskered man rode a large mule, his feet almost dragged the desert sands. The heat waves had made him look much taller as he rode across the dry lake bed. After unloading six sacks of ore on the depot platform Bill Pine, the station agent, told him that one of the sacks was badly torn and that he could not receive it for shipment in that condition. The old man returned to his pack outfit and brought another sack. When the torn sack was emptied out on the depot platform it almost started a stampede. The ore was a light gray iron-stained quartz literally plastered and matted together with bright yellow gold. Everyone crowded around to see the ore. Pete Ring exclaimed, "Jumping John D. Rockefeller, that's the richest ore that ever came out of the California desert!"

When the torn sack was emptied on the depot platform it almost started a stampede.

The old man gathered the ore up quickly, putting it in the new sack, weighed it and had the agent bill it to a San Francisco smelter. Some very rich gold ore was being hauled into Amboy at that time from a gold mine at Virginia Dale, operated by some Armenians from Los Angeles, but it was an entirely different kind of ore. While it showed considerable free gold, it was nothing to be compared with that brought in by the Hermit.

After watering his five burros and saddle mule at the tank car on the Santa Fe tracks, the old prospector went into camp just behind the little grocery store and near the railroad tracks. We all naturally wanted to know where the ore came from, but the old man was secretive and did not volunteer the information. In those days it was not considered good etiquette to inquire too closely into a stranger's personal affairs—especially if he happened to have a large six shooter handy.

The Armenian freighter told us the old prospector had been seen around their camp on several occasions and that they understood he was prospecting somewhere in that part of the desert. Later that evening the writer visited the old fellow around his campfire and found him reading the Psalms of David aloud from a large leather-covered Bible which he carried in his outfit.

He was worried because the other desert rats had seen his rich ore. He was afraid they would try to follow him to his mine.

He told me that while prospecting in the Sheep Hole mountains northeast of Dale dry lake and southwest of Cadiz dry lake, he had found an old Spanish or Mexican mine that showed evidence of having been worked hundreds of years before. An old arrastre nearby showed that the ore had been treated on the ground. However, there was no water other than a caved shaft near the arrastre that might have been a well. Two or three old graves nearby indicated that the former operators, or at least some of them, had been killed or died there. Old-time mining tools were scattered around.

During our conversation it developed that we had something in common. We were both from Kentucky. We proceeded to celebrate the occasion with a small nip or two from a bottle of Snake Medicine I happened to have in my hip pocket. After some talk the old man told me that he had done considerable prospecting around the desert, but that old Spanish shaft was the only deposit he had ever found that amounted to anything. The ore, he said, was enormously rich and there was enough in sight to make him wealthy beyond his fondest dreams. His description of the place would locate it either in the northeast corner of the Joshua Tree National Monument, or just across the line to the west. This area recently has been deleted from the monument boundaries.

During our conversation the prospector told me he had done some prospecting around a large outcropping of iron ore to the north of his mine, but that it was too lowgrade in gold to pay expenses of transportation and treatment.

Early the following morning when the Santa Fe passenger train pulled into the station the old fellow was observed to drop a letter in the slot in the mail car. The next morning, after watering his saddle mule and five burros he packed up, filled his numerous water kegs and followed one of the Armenian freight wagons out of town. No one ever saw or heard of him again. The letter probably instructed the smelter to mail the returns to some other postoffice or to family or friends in the east. He was never seen around Virginia Dale or any of the other railroad stations along the Santa Fe.

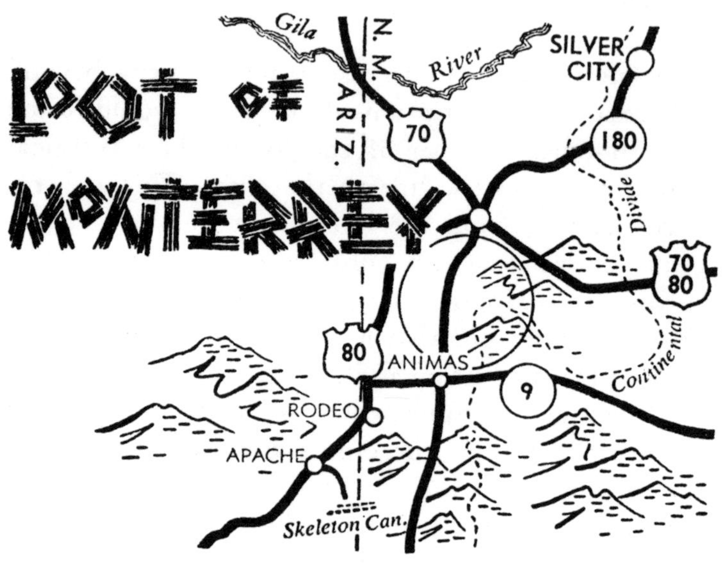

SOMEWHERE ALONG the old New Mexico trail that runs from Shakespeare to Skeleton canyon is a shallow mining shaft containing riches that would be quite astounding to the original owner of the prospect hole were he to return there.

According to the story current in this region, the original prospector found a small stringer of gold, but it pinched out before he had gone many feet beneath the surface—and the hole was abandoned. No one knows the location of this shaft, but today it is believed to contain 25 mule loads of gold and silver bars and buckskin bags of Spanish coins and jewelry.

The gold and silver bullion was stolen from the mint and smelter, and the jewels from the cathedral at Monterrey, Mexico. It is known as the "Monterrey loot," and for a time was buried in Skeleton canyon near the little town of Rodeo, New Mexico.

The bandit gang that stole the treasure and buried it was composed of Jim Hughes, Zwing Hunt, "Doc" Neal and Red Curley. Hughes was the leader, and he and his men were said to have been mixed up in the Lincoln county war in which Billy the Kid was the central figure.

Forming an alliance with the notorious Estrada gang, Hughes and his partners stole 25 U. S. government mules and then crossed the border into Mexico. They robbed the mint, smelter and cathedral at Monterrey and returned to United States territory with booty estimated to be worth $800,000. Shortly after returning to Texas, bad feeling developed between the Estrada men and the Hughes gang, and the feud ended in a gunfight in which the Mexicans were wiped out.

The treasure was buried temporarily in Skeleton canyon and Zwing Hunt, who had been wounded in the battle, was left to guard it. Other members of the band continued their raids on mining camps and stages in Arizona and New Mexico. Their last crime was the murder of a farmer and his son and the theft of their wagon and ox teams.

Hunt had recovered from his wound, and it was decided to load the treasure, which now amounted to over a million dollars, in the wagon and head for Silver City.

Two days from Skeleton canyon, a distance estimated between 40 and 50 miles, the unshod oxen became so crippled from travel over the sharp rocks they were unable to continue.

That night the loot was carried up a hill and dumped into the abandoned shaft. Two buckskin bags of jewelry and church plate were thrown in the hole on top of the money and bullion, and the shallow shaft filled with rocks and gravel from the dump. The oxen were turned loose to shift for themselves. The woodwork of the wagon was burned.

The bandits had taken what money they could carry conveniently, and when they reached Silver City they spent it freely. Heavy drinking led to a gunfight in which a young easterner was killed by one of the bandits, and the entire gang immediately dispersed to the hills with a posse after them. Neal was shot and died instantly. Hunt was wounded and taken to Tombstone where he subsequently escaped and was reported to have been killed by Apache Indians.

Red Curley and Hughes were overtaken and captured at Shakespeare where they were well known for their depredations, and both were hanged from a rafter in the dining room of the Pioneer House.

Curley offered to take his captors to the buried loot if the noose were taken from his neck, but the request was refused—and with his death none remained who knew the location of the treasure-filled mine shaft.

Prospectors have searched the area, and doodlebug gold hunters have made many trips into the region of Skeleton canyon and as far away as El Muerto springs—but the old shaft probably has acquired a covering of desert vegetation by now, and the recovery of the fortune is considered unlikely unless some one comes upon the spot by accident.

LOST TREASURE OF DEL BAC

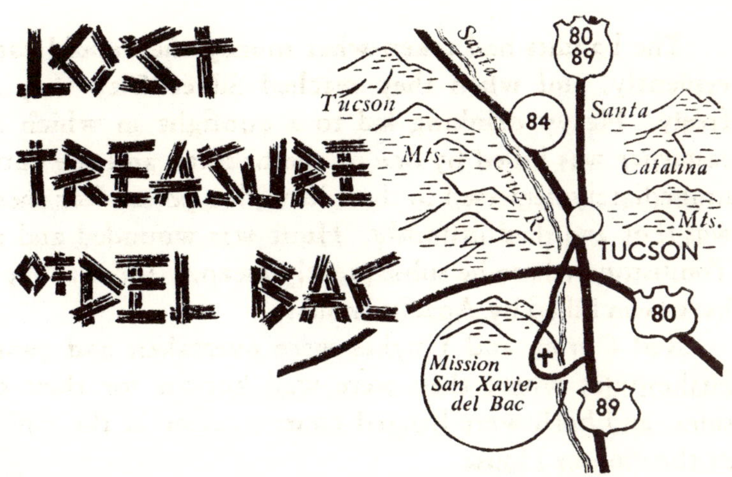

MANY LEGENDS cluster around the beautiful old mission of San Xavier del Bac, located on the west bank of the Santa Cruz river, a few miles south of Tucson, Arizona.

Father Eusebio Francisco Kino, the great Jesuit, wrote in his diary: "On April 28, 1700, we laid the foundation of a very spacious church." He told how the Indians had labored with pleasure and zeal in digging and in bringing stones from a nearby hill.

When the foundation of the church had been laid and the work of construction was well under way, the headmen of the Papagos begged Father Kino to go with them to a point in the mountains about two leagues to the southwest of Bac to see a rich vein of silver ore that had been discovered a few years before. It is related that the padre was well pleased with the rich outcropping. Noting its green color (horn silver) he called the lode *La Esmeralda* (The Emerald), and made arrangements to open the mine without delay.

The rich ore was mined and carried to the mission on the backs of Indians and smelted in a small adobe furnace built for the purpose.

Father Kino died March 15, 1711, at Magdalena, Sonora, where his remains rest in the old church, long since in ruins. After Kino's death the missions suffered through a number of minor revolts and constant attacks of the Apaches.

On the date of the first revolt of the Papago and Pima tribes in 1723, the treasure and silver ornaments on the altar at San Xavier del Bac were estimated to be worth more than 120,000 pesos. The loyal Papago neophytes secretly carried the treasure to the Esmeralda mine and buried it deep in the underground workings. In this revolt the churches at Bac, Tumacacori and Guevavi were partly destroyed and left without spiritual advisers.

In 1731 there came a small reinforcement of Jesuits. Two of them came north and effected what may be regarded as the first Spanish settlement in Arizona. Father Felipe Segesser took charge of San Xavier del Bac and Father Juan Baptista Grasshoffer of San Miguel de Guevavi, which at this time became a regular mission.

In 1733 and 1736 Father Carpar Steiger was at San Xavier del Bac and, in 1750, Father Jose Carucho.

In 1751 occurred the second revolt of the Pima tribes, in which Padres Francisco Xavier Saeta, Tomas Rollo and Enrique Ruen were killed and the missions at Sonoyta and Caborca were destroyed. Guevavi, Tumacacori and San Xavier del Bac were damaged and abandoned by all but a few loyal neophytes. In 1754 the Indians returned to their pueblos and stated that it was their desire to live peaceably. The great treasure was brought from the Esmeralda mine and placed on the altar and for a number of years San Xavier prospered greatly from agricultural, mining and stock raising industries and was considered one of the most flourishing of the long chain of missions established in Kino's time.

In 1767 King Charles issued his edict expelling all members of the Society of Jesus from Spain and its possessions. The Jesuits accepted their expulsion peacefully and after sealing the mines and burying their treasures made their way to the coast and the ships that were to take them away. After the departure of the Jesuits and before the Franciscans arrived to replace them, the long chain of beautiful missions again was partly, if not completely, abandoned and soon fell into ruin. San Xavier del Bac was partly destroyed but was not completely abandoned by its loyal Papago neophytes.

In 1783 Padre Carrillo was in charge of San Xavier del Bac and in that year he laid the foundations of the present mission, a structure still notable for its beautiful style of mission architecture.

Following the fall of the colonial government in 1822, the Franciscans departed and San Xavier del Bac and the Esmeralda mine were placed by the Bishop of Sonora under the charge of a secular priest at Magdalena. The faith had been well inculcated among the Papagos by the Jesuits and Franciscans, and the church and treasure had been jealously guarded and was almost intact in 1859 when the district was added to the diocese of New Mexico under Bishop Lamy.

San Xavier del Bac was the only mission in the long chain that was not in ruins. The Indians welcomed the priest with delight and rang the church bells with joy. Many of them remembered their prayers and a few of them were able to sing at Mass. The articles for the altar were again produced from the hiding place where they had lain for many years.

In 1860 many of the American miners who had been operating along the border since the close of the Mexican war and the signing of the Gadsden treaty, are said to have seen the treasure on the altar at San Xavier del Bac and estimated its value to be more than $60,000.

In 1861, when the American government withdrew the soldiers from Arizona to fight in the Civil war, the Apaches again started their raids on small mines and ranches, and the great treasure at San Xavier del Bac again disappeared. There is a tradition among the Indians around the old mission that the treasure still lies buried deep down in the old workings of the Esmeralda mine at the bottom of a large stope that has since caved in burying the silver under several hundred tons of rock and earth.

It is a singular fact that every year just before the fiesta of San Juan which occurs on June 24, the amount of rich silver ore brought to the ore buyers in Tucson and Nogales shows a marked increase. Most of this silver ore comes from two or three old Papagos who live on the banks of the Santa Cruz river near the mission. Many of the old time Mexicans who live near the river in Tucson, believe the ore comes from the dump and shallow surface workings of the Lost Esmeralda mine. It is understood in and around Tucson that many of the old Papagos know the location of the mine and treasure but refuse to disclose the information to anyone outside their tribe.

LOST NATIVE SILVER MINE

IN 1848, WHEN Major Heintzelman opened headquarters in Tubac in southern Arizona and started operations at the old Cerro Colorado silver mine located about 25 miles northwest of there, Opata Indians living in the vicinity frequently appeared at the store with large nuggets of native silver. No one knew where the Indians found the rich ore, but the supply seemed to be unlimited.

When the Apache Indians started raiding the small ranches and mining camps in southern Arizona, the Opatas ceased making their prospecting trips to the south of the Tumacacori mission and Tubac and remained close to the post which was protected by soldiers. The mines were forced to close in the early sixties when the soldiers were withdrawn to fight in the Civil war.

For a long period none of the silver nuggets were seen. Then one day in the early '80s an old prospector walked into the saloon and gambling house of John Connors in Nogales and laid a large piece of native silver on the bar. Connors had been a miner for a number of years and had done some prospecting on his own account and immediately recognized the silver specimen as being valuable. The old prospector, when questioned by Connors, stated that he purchased the nugget from an old Opata Indian living up on the Santa Cruz river near the little town of Tubac.

The Indian said the nugget had been picked up by him while hunting deer along Carrizo creek south of the Tascosa mountains and that there was much more where that came from. This Indian farmer evidently did not think the nugget was valuable, for he sold it for a few dollars. Connors purchased the specimen and agreed to grubstake the old prospector for a trip into the Carrizo creek country to search for the source of the silver.

The Apache Indians were on the warpath again and Connors, realizing the danger of sending an old man out alone on a long trip, induced him to take a younger man along. The two set out with their burros and camp outfit and were not heard from for several weeks. Then the younger man grew tired and returned alone to Nogales.

Weeks and months passed and then one day the old man appeared with his four burros loaded down with ore that was almost pure silver. The prospector told Connors that after the younger man left he prospected farther along Carrizo creek toward the Mexican line and found the ground sprinkled with the large nuggets which had evidently eroded from an outcropping of kaolin (called *caliche* by the Indians and Mexicans).

After having the silver assayed Connors divided the returns equally between the old man and himself and made the necessary arrangements to return to the location and work the rich find.

The old man, elated over his sudden good fortune, spent his money freely at the bars and gambling tables, and on the day set for the departure for the mine he failed to appear. A searching party was started, and the dead body of the prospector was discovered back of a warehouse owned by Connors. It had been a cold night, and he had died from effects of drink and exposure.

Connors made several trips to the Carrizo creek country but was unable to find any trace of the silver nuggets or the kaolin outcrop from which they evidently had eroded. The famous Planchas de Plata silver mine is located just across the border in Sonora and only a few miles south of the spot where the nuggets were reported to have been found by the old man. It is a historical fact that at the Planchas de Plata many nuggets of native silver were found by the Spaniards. One nugget weighed 2700 pounds. Many others weighed from 25 to 250 pounds each. But the source of the four burro loads of rich ore remains to this day a secret shrouded in mystery.

LOST GOLD OF THE GUADALUPES

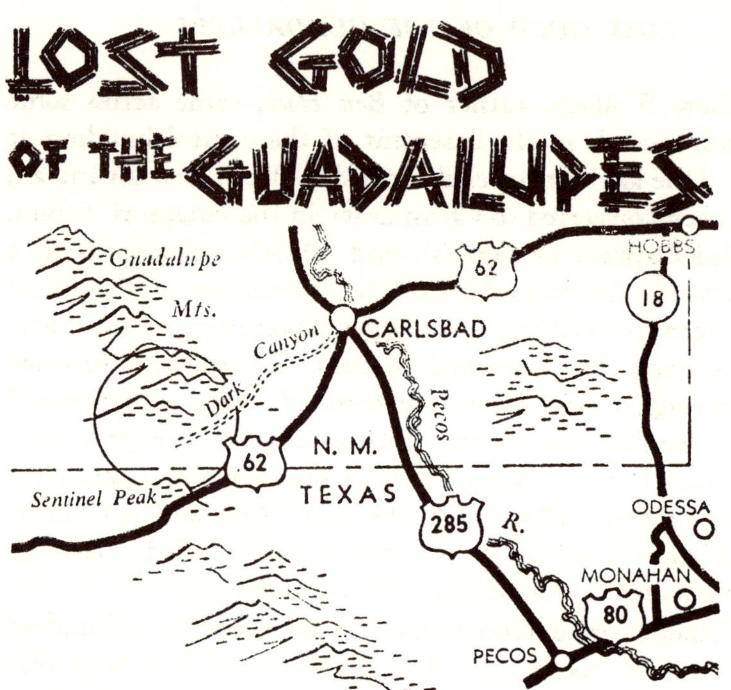

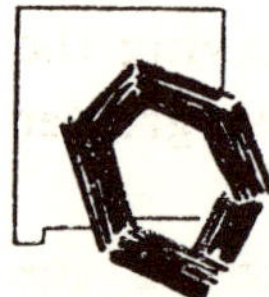LD GERONIMO, notorious Apache leader, once said that the richest gold mines in the United States lay hidden in the Guadalupes.

Sentinel peak in northwest Texas, a short distance south of the New Mexico state line, rises to a height of 9500 feet above sea level and is the highest point of land in the Lone Star state. This magnificent mountain peak near the south end of the Guadalupe range has for many years been a friendly guidepost to prospectors and adventurers searching for a lost mine somewhere to the north of the peak and west of the Pecos river.

While he was governor of the Territory of New Mexico,

General Lew Wallace, author of *Ben Hur,* came across some old Spanish records in the basement of the capitol building at Santa Fe. One ancient paper described in detail how an Indian, who had been converted to Christianity in the village of Tabira, had guided Captain de Gavilan and 30 other Spaniards to a point known as Sierra de las Cenizas (mountain of the ashes) on the eastern spurs of the Guadalupes. According to the document, the party had returned to Santa Fe heavily burdened with gold nuggets and ore in the form of "wires and masses." Shortly thereafter the Pueblo Indians started the great uprising in which every Spaniard who did not flee from New Mexico was killed. This was in the year 1680, and the village of Tabira was wiped out and the Indian guide killed. Sierra de las Cenizas joined the long list of lost mines.

The Guadalupes extend from Sentinel peak for a hundred miles or more to the north. The dark-colored lava beds that make up the greater part of the formation are gashed by deep narrow canyons or crevices through which flood waters from the mountains are carried to the Pecos river. After leaving the Pecos, water is scarce, as the canyons are dry for the greater part of the year.

Grapevine spring in Dark canyon to the north of the Carlsbad caverns furnishes a small amount of water the whole year 'round. The spring takes its name from what is probably the largest grapevine in the state. This vine climbs up the almost vertical wall to a height of several hundred feet. It is to this spring that the herders bring their Angora goats for water and to bed down for the night. A short distance to the west of Grapevine spring a jet of water the size of a man's arm spouts from the canyon wall during several months of the year.

It was through this dangerous canyon that the Spaniards carried their gold to the Pecos river and thence down to the City of Mexico. All of the pack trains did not get through. The bones of many soldiers still may be seen on the high mesa just north of Grapevine spring. Eighteen jack loads of virgin gold were said to have been buried near the spring just before a fight with the Indians took place.

During the construction of the Texas and Pacific railroad, old Ben Sublett pitched his tent near a section house where the town of Monahan now stands. For several years he did odd jobs along the railroad and prospected for gold in the Indian-infested Guadalupes to the north. Then one day old Ben showed up in Monahan with a small sack of gold nuggets and announced in a saloon that he had struck it rich. The drinks were on the house.

After that old Ben devoted his entire time to prospecting and made frequent trips into the Guadalupes, each time returning with a small sack of gold nuggets. He seemed well supplied with money and spent it freely around Monahan and Odessa, Texas. However, no amount of persuasion on the part of his friends or of the townspeople would induce the wily old prospector to disclose the source of his wealth.

Sublett died in 1892 at the age of 82 years and was buried in Odessa. He left no map or waybill to his mine.

I doubt if there is a man in Texas or New Mexico who has not heard the story of Sublett's mine. Hundreds of adventurers and prospectors have searched the Guadalupes from one end to the other, from north to south, from east to west. From old Fort Sumner, New Mexico, to the mouth of the Pecos down on the Rio Grande the story is as fresh today as it was when

Sublett's son claims to have a distinct recollection of his father taking him to the mine.

Ben first showed up with his sack of nuggets and announced that, finally after many years, he had struck it rich.

Sublett's son, Ross, now living in Carlsbad, New Mexico, claims to have a distinct recollection of his father having taken him to the mine when he was a very small boy and having seen his father climb down a rope ladder into a crevice and bring out gold nuggets. He says there was a tunnel at one end of this crevice or open cut. He was too young to take any interest in it at the time, but he has spent many years since the death of his father trying to find his way back to the mine.

Lost mines located in a wild Indian country are always rich. The wilder the Indians the richer the mines seem to be. Sierra de las Cenizas and old Ben Sublett's mine are no exception to the rule. But both mines seem to have disappeared completely from the face of the earth.

Not so with the 18 jack loads of virgin gold buried at Grapevine spring in Dark canyon. Herders tending their flocks of Angora goats at the spring in the rainy season say strange lights suddenly leap out of the ground among the oaks that line the canyon wall just across from the spring and below the high mesa where are the graves of the Spanish soldiers. This Dark canyon country is a land of ghost stories, and the old goat herders who graze their flocks on the rocky rattlesnake-infested mesas say that on dark windy nights, the old captain and his soldiers rise from their graves, mount their mules and gallop up and down the rocky canyon where the 18 jack loads of virgin gold lie buried, then, like the strange lights, vanish into the darkness as suddenly as they came.

Whether Sierra de las Cenizas and the Sublett mine are one and the same, it is impossible to say. There is a Sierra de las Cenizas in the eastern part of the state of Sonora, Mexico, where 500 Indians and Mexican *gambucinos* have for a long time been making their living by picking large gold nuggets out of conglomerate that has formed around this small mountain of the ashes. If Sierra de las Cenizas in the Guadalupes is as rich as its namesake across the line, it would seem to be well worth looking for.

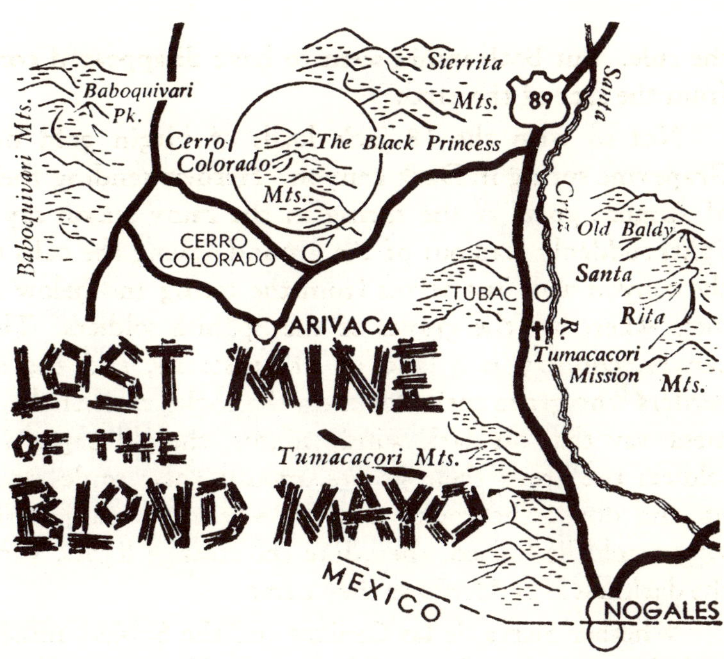

TEN MILES NORTHEAST of the old mining town of Arivaca, Arizona, half way between Baboquivari peak to the west and Old Baldy or *El Pelon*, stands the Black Princess, a natural rock formation carved by wind and sand to resemble the body of a woman lying outstretched on top of the highest ridge in the Cerro Colorado mountains. Vividly outlined against the sky, the Black Princess glows and gleams in the sunset and looks so realistic that she has long been held sacred by the Opata and Papago Indians.

In winter she is feared. On wild stormy nights when the wind howls down across the Catalina and Sierrita mountains, lightning leaps from the black clouds that settle down over the head and shoulders of the Black Princess and eerily silhouette her form against the sky. Thunder rolls back and forth across the steep canyon walls, rain comes down in sheets and swirls that loosen huge boulders from the steep mountainsides, hurling them into the raging torrents to be left stranded on the floor of the desert below. Wild boars seek shelter from the raging elements in the dark caves under the shelving lava flows, and giant jaguars from the Moche Cowie country in Sonora stalk their prey around the few rock tanks and the one natural spring that bubbles from under the tufa beds on the north side of the mountain.

But when spring comes, the Black Princess looks down serenely from the mountaintop upon desert plains brilliantly carpeted with wildflowers. The sun, setting behind the ragged edge of the Baboquivari range, crowns her with gleaming gold. When the moon comes up over the Santa Rita mountains and sheds its long rays of silvery light down across the Sierrita and Cerro Colorado mountains, and the desert breezes begin to stir, the snow-white yucca blossoms that cluster around the feet of the Black Princess become swaying ghosts with fleecy veils.

There are many legends about the Black Princess mountain. Perhaps the most interesting is the tale of the lost gold mine of the Blond Mayo Indian.

It was in 1861, about the time the United States government withdrew its troops from Arizona to fight in the Civil war, that the two Mayo Indian brothers, Juan Morales, the blond, and Fermin, his younger brother, came to the Arivaca country from the Mayo valley in southern Sonora. Upon the departure of the troops, the Apaches and Mexican bandits again renewed their raids on small mines and out-lying ranches, and the pioneers were gathering in Tucson and Arivaca for protection. John Poston, superintendent of the Silver Queen mine at Cerro Colorado, and a number of his employes had just been murdered by Mexican bandits from Sonora. Upon the grave of John Poston and many others, both American and Mexican, the men of Arivaca swore the Vendetta—the "Vengeance of the West"—and kept it.

The two Morales brothers, Juan, locally called *El Guero Mayo,* and Fermin made their living panning placer along Arivaca creek and on the surrounding mesas which were rich in gold. In the course of time the Blond Mayo quit his panning operations and made many trips into the surrounding country. He seemed to be searching for something. One day he came into camp from a northeasterly direction, his six pack mules loaded with rich gold ore. The quartz was matted together with wire and masses of bright yellow gold and had a blue indigo tinge, probably bromide of silver. The ore looked as though it had been mined more than a hundred years before. Adhering to many of the pieces were small bits of a porous lava rock suggesting that it might have come from one of those rare pipes or chimneys found in lava flows. Wherever found in any part of the world these pipes or chimneys have produced millions in gold.

The Blond Mayo made many weekly trips into the northeast end of the district in the vicinity of the Black Princess, always returning with his six pack mules heavily loaded. The rich gold ore was treated in arrastres that still stand on the north side of Arivaca creek about three miles west of town.

On these weekly trips to and from his mine, *El Guero Mayo,* like young Lochinvar of King Arthur's court, "rode all alone and through all the wide border his steed was the best." However, unlike the gay young knight, he did not ride unarmed. Across the pommel of his silver-mounted saddle rested a long rifle, and from the two well-filled cartridge belts around his slender waist dangled a pair of heavy Colt revolvers. The Blond Mayo was a dead shot; the way he picked off an Apache chief or buck at long range was a continual source of wonderment to his many friends as well as to the tribespeople back in the hills awaiting the return of the victim. He was gaunt, eagle-eyed, tireless and remorseless as doom when it came to avenging the death of a friend at the hands of an Apache. He rode the high ridges and the skyline, as Indians do, avoiding as much as possible the narrow passes and the mesquite-choked washes where an ambush might be laid against him.

Old timers in Arivaca, like Don Manuel Gonzales and Don Teofilio Ortiz, who knew the Blond Mayo when they were young men, say that normally he was quiet and stayed away from strong drink. But occasionally, when he received an extraordinarily large return on his ore, he went on a rampage —a "ramtooch" they called it. On these rare occasions he came into town six guns blazing at the sky and yelling like a Comanche Indian. The sound of his horse's clattering hoofs and the roar of his guns were signals for all the little brown *muchachitos* and some of the older ones to rush into the dusty street to scramble for the handfuls of silver coins that *El Guero Mayo* would throw at their feet.

Arivaca was a wild camp in those days, filled to overflowing with mule-skinners, bullwhackers, miners, *gambucinos,* vaqueros, saloonkeepers, tin horn gamblers, and dance hall girls. Money was plentiful, the people were happy despite the raids of marauding Indians, and *bailes,* fandangos and fiestas were held with or without provocation.

As the years passed, the Morales brothers prospered from their mining operations along the creek and back in the hills.

Fermin, the younger brother, ran cattle on the Calera ranch three miles north of town, and *El Guero Mayo* established a cattle ranch on the Batamonte wash below the Black Princess mountain, presumably to keep an eye on his bonanza gold mine.

While the brothers were somewhat secretive when it came to discussing their private affairs, it is believed by many Hispano-Arizonans around Arivaca that they came north for the express purpose of locating and working this rich gold mine. There is much evidence to show that the mine—perhaps the old Sopori mine—was first discovered by the Jesuits or other Spaniards that came north in the wake of the Coronado expedition searching for the Seven Golden Cities of Cibola. Old Spanish and early American maps show the Sopori mine in the vicinity of the Black Princess mountain. Many people confuse it with the old Isabelle shaft located one and one-half miles south of the Sopori ranch house. The Isabelle was worked by the Jesuit fathers from the Tumacacori mission.

An old volume in the Arizona State library at Phoenix reports: "The Sopori mine was known all over Arizona and Sonora for the richness of its ores." The ruins of an old adobe smelting furnace on the arroyo west of the Black Princess and the walls of an old mission that stand on a long point of land jutting out into the Altar valley east of Baboquivari peak would seem to indicate that the mine was known to and worked by the people who lived around this mission, perhaps by the priests and their Indian neophytes. The name of the mission has been lost. It may not have been a full-ranking mission, but a *visita* or a halfway station on the trail from other missions in western Sonora, where the padres stopped to rest and say Mass on their way to San Xavier del Bac, Tumacacori, Guevavi and Cocospra, all on the Santa Cruz river south of Tucson.

When old and full of years, *El Guerro Mayo* died while on a visit to his old home in the Rio Mayo valley in Sonora, Mexico. Fermin, the younger brother, died in Arivaca about 20 years ago and lies buried in the old Campo Santo on the north edge of the town.

Lester Fernstrom, a tungsten miner in the Arizona district for many years, flew his plane over the Black Princess mountain a few years ago and reported having seen a long open cut on the side of the mountain. The cut was choked with huge boulders and could well be the entrance to the Blond Mayo's mine. The Indian was never known to have carried any explosives or mining tools with him to or from his mine, and those who knew him agree that he probably found the ore already mined by the former operators. The fact that the ore brought to the arrastres showed no fresh surfaces would seem to bear this out.

Mere mention of the Blond Mayo's name in Arivaca invariably starts a discussion of his lost mine. But it is all speculation. No one yet has located the bonanza which supplied his mules with their rich loads. The old Indians and the Black Princess guard their secret well.

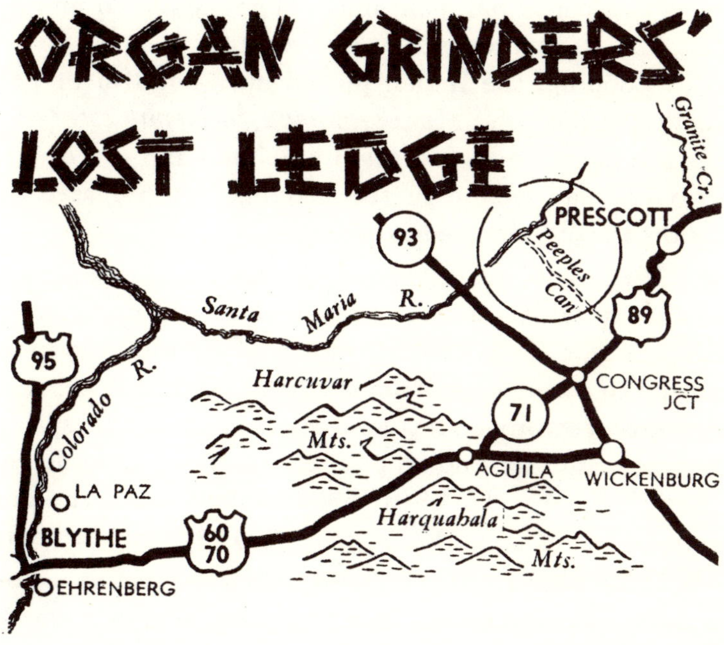

THE LATE BILL BEAR, an old-time Arizona prospector, trapper and squaw man, is authority for the following story:

"In the early sixties," said Bill, "three Italian organ grinders each with a hand organ and a trained monkey traveling from La Paz on the Colorado river to Granite creek near Prescott, Arizona, turned aside from the trail one day to rest in the shade of a mesquite tree.

"Here they found an old Indian lying down, wearied and almost dead from thirst and heat. They shared the contents of their canteen with him and gave him food from their meager supply. Grateful for their kindness, the old Mojave offered to show them a rich gold mine. They hesitated and questioned him as to its richness and probable value.

"Stooping, the Indian picked up a handful of pebbles and replied in Spanish, '*Mucho, mucho, lo mismo esta,*' as he swept his arm outward, to indicate its richness and extent. The organ grinders required no further urging, but prepared at once to follow the old Mojave into the hills.

"Two days' travel across the burning sands brought them to the Santa Maria river and on the third day they reached a deep canyon up in the hills north of Peeples' canyon. A small stream of clear water trickled from under a big rock and two or three cottonwood trees grew by the little spring. After making camp the Indian pointed westward and said laconically, '*Busca*' (hunt). He then threw himself upon the ground and rolled a cigarette, as if that were the only interest he had in life.

"The three Italians hurried westward and at a point a few hundred yards distance in a tributary arroyo a small ledge of dark colored rock arrested their attention. They broke off a piece which glistened in the afternoon sunlight. It was thickly studded with gold. The yellow metal seemed to be present, sparkling and glittering, wherever they broke the rock. They sat down and gazed at the golden treasure, then broke off more, reveling in dreams of riches. Not until the evening shadows crept down upon them did they return to their campfire.

"The old Mojave lay sleeping, but little sleep came to the three Italians during the long night. On the morrow they filled several small bags with pieces of quartz and golden nuggets from the ledge where it outcropped in the wash and then prepared to leave. They had little food with them and intended to return as soon as possible to dig out their fortunes.

Stooping, the old Indian picked up a handful of pebbles and replied in Spanish: "Mucho, mucho lo mismo esta," as he swept his arm outward to indicate the ore's richness and extent.

"They covered up the ledge and after marking the locality well, drew a rough map of the place, noting a few of the most prominent landmarks and plainly marking the trail leading from the Santa Maria river. As the sun sank low over the western hills they started back, preferring to travel by night to avoid an attack by the Hualapais, enemies of the Mojaves. The little party reached Tres Alamos springs in safety, resting there overnight. They planned to start early the next morning for Wickenburg, which was the nearest town. Just before the faint glow of dawn streaked the east, a hideous yell startled the tired sleepers. Three or four Hualapai Indians sprang upon them killing the Mojave and two of the Italians. The third Italian, for the moment screened by some thick bushes, made his escape. After killing the three men the Indians left the scene hastily, evidently fearing pursuit by the soldiers from Camp Date which was not far away.

"When the Indians had gone the lone Italian returned and placed the bodies of his three friends together and after piling dry brush over them, he set fire to the funeral pyre. Then he put the crude map and a written page in a small metal box from one of the hand organs and buried it under a large boulder near the little spring.

"Gathering up the bags of gold and filling one of the canteens with water, he set out on the long journey across the parched desert in the direction of Wickenburg. The three little monkeys were released at the spring to shift for themselves as best they could.

"Two days later Francisco Gonzales, a teamster making his way across the desert from Weaver creek to Wickenburg, found the unfortunate Italian lying face down in the sand by the side of the road clutching the bags of gold in his hands and almost dead from thirst. He was placed in the wagon and after being given some water the Italian revived sufficiently to tell his story in broken Spanish, but died before reaching Wickenburg.

"The ledge has not been found."

LOST GOLDEN EAGLE MINE

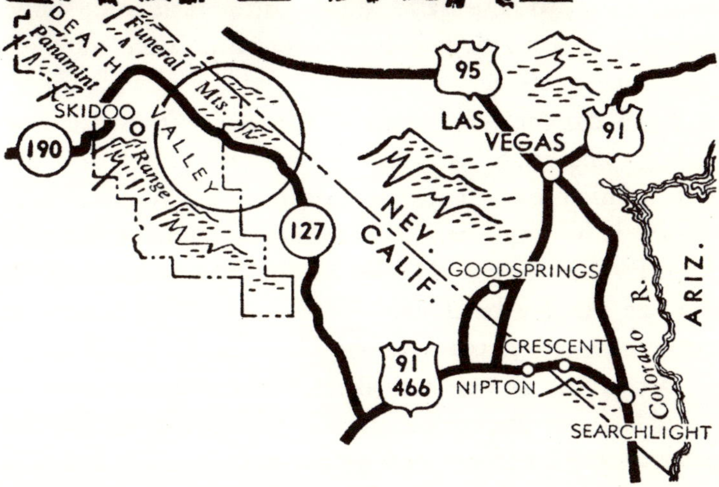

IT WAS IN THE summer of 1902 that Alkali Jones, old-time prospector and desert rat, set out across the desert from Skidoo, California to Searchlight, Nevada. His route lay across one of the hottest and most desolate regions in the United States—Death Valley. For centuries it has been known to the Shoshone Indians, as *To-me-sha* (Ground on fire). Alkali was in a hurry to reach Searchlight, and he was traveling with one pack burro. He carried a .22 calibre rifle, a small prospecting pick, five pounds of jerky, five pounds of bacon, some hardtack, coffee, sugar, salt, a small frying pan, coffee pot and an old army kit. This, together with a gallon canteen of water and his bedroll, made a total pack load of less than 100 pounds.

Two days after leaving Skidoo, while crossing a narrow arm of the valley, he was caught suddenly in a fierce sandstorm. The sun hung like a copper disk in the darkened sky and the wind whipped the sand dunes into fantastic shapes. Small particles of sand driven by the terrific force of the wind cut like points of steel.

Semi-darkness fell, and as the weary traveler stumbled on through the sand his attention was attracted to a dark object that loomed only a short distance ahead. Making his way toward it he soon came to the foot of a small butte that stood alone in the desert. At the base of the butte were a number of huge granite boulders. These seemed to offer some shelter from the raging storm, so he made camp beside one of them.

When the storm had abated and the sun came out again Jones left his shelter beside the huge granite boulder and, in order to get a better view of the surrounding country, started to climb toward the summit of the little butte. When about half way up the north side his attention was attracted to some pieces of a milky white quartz that lay scattered along the hillside. With the small pick that he carried in his belt he broke several pieces of the quartz and found it to be matted together with large stringers of bright yellow gold.

Running along the side of the hill in a northeasterly and southwesterly direction was a white quartz vein about three feet wide. It outcropped for a distance of about one thousand feet before it disappeared under the sand at the foot of the little granite butte. The vein was a fissure in pink granite and showed free gold wherever it was broken open.

Alkali took a location notice from a pouch he carried at

his belt. While engaged in filling it out he looked up into the sky and saw a huge bird wheeling high over head. It was so far above him he was unable to tell whether it was an eagle or a huge California condor that was dogging his footsteps waiting for a chance to pick the meat from his bones. At any rate, he called his claim the "Golden Eagle." When he had finished the location notice he signed his name to it and then placed it in an empty tobacco can. Then he gathered up about 10 pounds of the rich white quartz and placed it in a small sample sack. From the loose quartz and rock scattered on the hillside he built a monument and placed the tin can containing the location notice in it.

It was getting late in the afternoon when Jones climbed down from the little butte and headed for the higher mountains to the north. After traveling a distance of about one mile he came to the foot of the mountains and started climbing. When a few thousand feet up he sat down to rest. The map in his pocket showed that he was in the Funeral range sitting on Coffin mountain looking down into Death Valley. He had only one pint of water left in his canteen.

As he sat there making a crude map of the location of his mine, the valley below him suddenly filled with water. It danced and sparkled in the evening sunlight as the gentle waves broke into spray against the pink granite butte and the great boulders at its base. Beautiful trees and fairy castles appeared along the shore. Jones, being a man of the desert, knew the lake was only another of the enticing mirages that had lured hundreds of less experienced men to horrible death on the burning sands.

So, instead of heading out into the desert waste to search for water, he turned his footsteps toward the Funeral range.

When he had traveled a distance of about two miles he came to a deep canyon. Pausing on the brink, he looked into the canyon bed far below. As he stood there he saw doves, quail and whitewings in pairs and small flocks flying swiftly up the canyon. This he knew to be a sure sign of water not far away. Climbing down into the deep canyon he continued to walk along its bed for a distance of about a mile and then suddenly came to a large tank that nature had scooped out of the solid bedrock. It was full of clear water and was surrounded by thousands of quail and other birds. A small bed of sand under a shelving rock in the nearby canyon wall offered an ideal place to camp for the night. Jones could have killed some of the quail or whitewings for his supper, but he did not have the heart to destroy the friends who had saved his life by leading him to their secret watering place. When he had filled himself with jerky, hardtack and coffee he lay down in the warm sand to rest.

Little sleep came to Alkali Jones that night. He lay awake reveling in the dreams of bonanza. The wail of a coyote came up from the desert and owls hooted from the crags above the waterhole. From high up among the rocks a bobcat screamed his challenge across the canyon, but only the echo came back.

Jones prepared a breakfast of bacon, hardtack and coffee and was well on his way down the east side of the Funeral range with his canteen full of fresh water and the 10 pound bag of rich ore clutched in his hand when the first rays of dawn tinted the east and Death Valley was again flooded with golden sunlight.

After leaving the Funeral mountains Jones passed into the Amargosa range and camped the next night on Amargosa river. From there he made his way southeast to Charleston mountain, Goodsprings, Crescent and Searchlight. Upon his arrival at Searchlight he took about one pound of the rich quartz and had it assayed. It ran $41,000 in gold to the ton. The remaining nine pounds were ground up in a mortar and returned $180,000 in gold. With the money so obtained Jones purchased three burros from Winfield Sherman, a desert character well known in Crescent and Searchlight. At a store in Searchlight he purchased provisions and mining tools. He then wrote his sister in the east and was ready to return to the Death Valley country to work his mine.

While in the mining town of Searchlight, Jones took his meals at Jack Wheatley's eating house, and it was there that the writer saw the wonderful ore and heard the story direct from Jones' own lips.

Three days later Jones loaded his outfit on two of the burros, mounted the third and set out across the cactus-covered flats in the direction of Crescent peak. That was the last his friends ever saw of him. It was learned later by his sister, who came west to search for him, that he spent the night at the Gus Halfpenny gold mine on the west side of Crescent peak and a few days later passed through Goodsprings headed for the Death Valley country.

The years passed and no word of Alkali Jones or his Golden Eagle mine ever came out of the desert. Then one day two old Shoshone Indians making their way across the desert along the east side of the Funeral range came upon the scattered remnants of a weathered pack outfit under a large mesquite tree. Scattered in the sand were some old rusty mining tools, but the body of Jones was nowhere to be found. He is believed to have run out of water somewhere on the desert between the Amargosa river and the eastern foothills of the Funeral range and to have started out on foot to find the tank of the friendly birds where he had camped only a few weeks before. Either he met with some accident or was overtaken by heat and thirst. The burros no doubt eventually joined the wild herds which roam that region.

Jones' Golden Eagle mine may have met the fate which is known to have overtaken more than one rich deposit in the Death Valley region, where winds of hurricane velocity sweep across the desert at certain seasons of the year. These winds carry great volumes of sand and may pile up a drift many feet in depth within a week's time.

But the same winds which often cover rich ore deposits may sooner or later expose them to view again, and there is always the possibility that a prospector may come upon a rich claim in a region previously trod by other gold-seekers.

TWO SUNS EAST

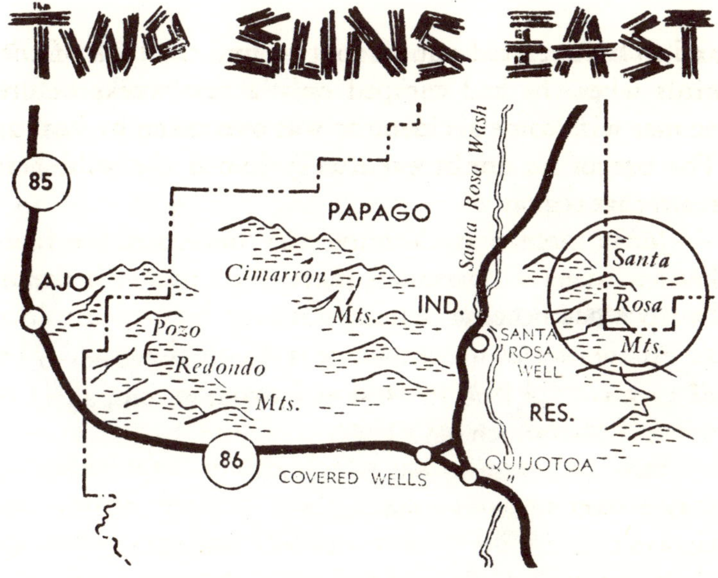

ABOUT 75 MILES, or two suns, as an Indian measures distance, east of Ajo, Arizona, near the eastern edge of the Santa Rosa country, is a rich gold ledge or chimney running thousands of dollars to the ton. Many Indians now living knew the old Papago who found and for a time worked the mine. When in need of money with which to buy food for himself and family the old man would leave the village early in the morning and always return before dark with a small sack full of rich gold ore which he gave to his squaw to grind in the metate to free the gold from the rock. The gold was then sold or traded to merchants in Casa Grande, Gila Bend or Ajo.

Many years passed and the old man made frequent trips to the mine, each time returning with a sack of rich gold ore. When too old and feeble to travel any more he told his grandson about the mine and how to find it. The entrance was always kept covered with a large flat rock. Eventually the old man died, leaving his grandson in sole possession of the secret.

A drouth came upon the Indian country and food and money were scarce, so the young Indian set out to find the mine. He made many trips to the mountain in which the old man said the mine was located, but no trace of it could he find. The rock had become covered with earth.

The young Indian came to Ajo and appealed to the writer for assistance to find the mine. He was accompanied by an old Indian. The youth said the trip could be made on mules in two suns. The route led out across the Ajo valley and then up over the old Indian trail to a large tank of clear water near the summit of the first range of mountains. Thousands of quail, doves and many kinds of wild animals come to this natural tank for water in the dry season when many waterholes in the desert dry up.

It was about noon when we reached the tank. The mules were hobbled in a small patch of grass, and while the coffee was bubbling and the fresh meat that we had brought along for our first meal was roasting on a bed of coals, a large coyote, attracted by the smell of meat, appeared on top of a small hill a short distance away. I picked up my 30-30 rifle and was about to shoot the predator when the old Indian laid his hand on my arm and asked me not to do so. Curious to know why he did not want the animal shot, I asked him to explain. He replied that it might be his grandmother. An Indian believes that after death the spirit of his grandmother comes back to earth in the form of a coyote.

Thinking to have some fun at the old man's expense, I told him that a white man believes that it is the spirit of his mother-in-law that returns to earth after death in the form of a coyote. He hung his head and looked serious for a moment, as if recalling some unpleasant incident in his past life, and finally looked up and replied if that was right to go ahead and shoot. Not being quite sure myself and having no desire to shoot either of his relatives, I lowered the rifle and let the animal go.

From the tank the trail led up over the summit of a high ridge and down into a beautiful valley carpeted with tall grass and many kinds of wildflowers. In the center of this valley stands a small tabletop mountain. Thousands of dead Papagos lie buried in the loose rock around its base. The older Indian was bothered with ear ache and we had to stop occasionally to allow the younger Indian to pour a can of water in the old man's ear. To this day I have never been able to figure out where the water went to. It all went in and none came out.

We reached the village of Many Wells late the second day and passed the night in a small brush house, or "hookie" as they call it. There were eight people and half as many dogs, all sleeping on the floor. When one wanted to turn over, we all turned.

Two day's search failed to disclose the location of the mine itself, but a large piece of float picked up in an arroyo on the west side of the mountain weighed 35 pounds and, when broken up, was found to contain $1200 worth of gold. The young Papago insists, and perhaps correctly, that the rich gold ledge is located in that small iron-stained mountain just two suns east of Ajo.

LOST YUMA LEDGE

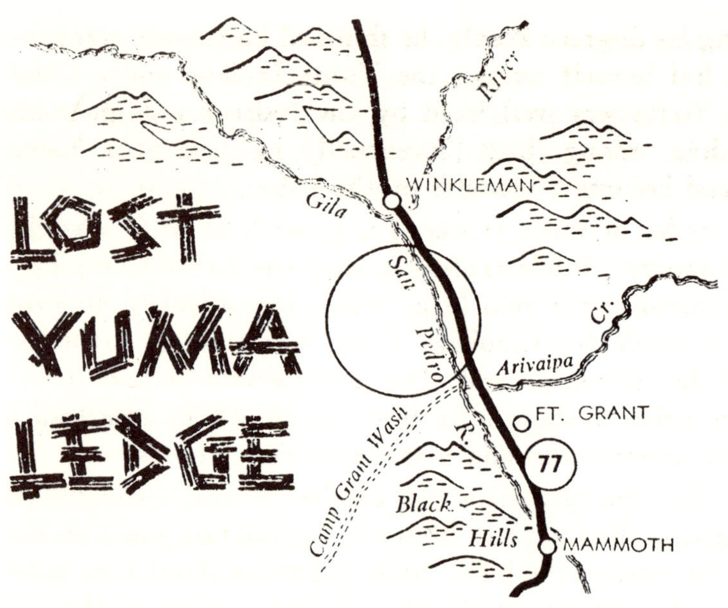

A BADLY RUSTED COLT revolver such as was used by army and frontiersmen in the early days on the border was recently found in the Arivaipa country near old Fort Grant. It is believed by many to be a clue to the lost Yuma gold ledge said to have been discovered by Apache Indians long before old Geronimo and his band of braves were rounded up and placed on a reservation.

The outcropping of rich gold ore was once shown to a graduate of West Point whose real name seems to have been lost somewhere in the mystic reaches of the past. He is remembered only as "Yuma" on account of having at one time been acting quartermaster at the post at Fort Yuma on the Colorado river. Because of irregularities in his accounts the officer was courtmartialed and discharged from the army.

Feeling his disgrace keenly, he shunned his former companions and hid himself among the Yuma Indians under Chief Pascual. Yuma was well liked by the Indians and spent his time trading among them. Eventually he married a Yuma woman and became a member of the tribe.

As a trader he made frequent trips with his wife into the Apache country. While trading among the Arivaipa Apaches he heard rumors of a gold ledge where the Apaches obtained rich ore to trade for supplies. Yuma was eager to learn the secret of the rich ledge and after considerable persuasion induced the chief to show it to him. In return he promised a rifle, some ammunition and a few trinkets.

Soon after the agreement was reached Yuma, accompanied by the Apache chief, set out from the Apache camp in a northerly direction across the hills. After traveling about nine miles they reached a ridge between the San Pedro river on the east and a deep rocky canyon which terminated a short distance to the west of where they were standing.

Before them in a crater-like depression was an outcropping of rose quartz rich in coarse gold. With his hunting knife Yuma broke off a handful of the brittle ore that gleamed yellow in the morning sunlight. After securing samples the outcrop was carefully covered with dirt and rocks until no sign of the ore remained on the surface. Yuma was not a miner, but he realized that the quartz was very rich. Also, he knew it was guarded by Indians who would kill him on sight if they ever found him there again.

After remaining in the Arivaipa country a few days Yuma went to Tucson where he showed the ore to a man by the name of Crittenden whom he had known as a freighter when he was in the army post at Yuma. Yuma and Crittenden decided to return to the Arivaipa country and explore the mine and sample it more thoroughly. Accordingly they set out from the old pueblo of Tucson late one afternoon and after riding all night they arrived early the next morning at Fort Grant.

They refreshed themselves, fed and watered the horses and that afternoon rode north down the San Pedro river. After traveling about 10 miles they made camp in the brush along the river and waited for morning. When the first rays of light appeared in the east they started to climb the steep mountain-side toward the west. The terrain was rough and they were forced to lead their mounts most of the way. They soon came to the long ridge overlooking the river and the deep box canyon.

They found the quartz ledge and with a pick dug out 25 or 30 pounds of the rich ore. Putting the ore in a sack they covered the ledge again and hid the pick. Taking a last look around to make sure no Indians were in the vicinity they headed their horses down the steep rocky trail toward the west and out into the cactus covered desert below. They rode all that night and arrived in Tucson early the next morning without having seen any of the Apaches.

The sack of ore that they brought out was crushed in a mortar and produced $1200 worth of gold. Knowing the Apaches were on the warpath and that it would be extremely dangerous to undertake any development work at that time, Yuma resumed his trading and Crittenden continued his freighting operations between the mines and the post at Yuma on the Colorado.

Yuma loaded his pack mules with supplies and with his Indian wife set out across the desert toward the Papago country. That was the last ever seen of them by their friends. There is a story among the Papago Indians at Ajo that Yuma and his

Taking a last look around to make sure no Indians were in the vicinity, they headed their horses down the steep mountainside toward the west.

wife were killed by a band of renegade Apache Indians whom they met in the Growler pass north of Quitobaquita. They were buried by the Papagos, and the piles of rocks marking the graves may still be seen just a few hundred feet west of the old road that leads through the Growler pass and on down to Cipriano wells near the border.

When Yuma and his wife failed to return to Tucson after several months, Crittenden, believing them to have met with foul play, decided to return to the mine alone. Mounted on a fine horse he left Tucson early one morning and after riding all that day and far into the night he arrived at Fort Grant where he rested for a few days. He revealed his plans to the officers at the fort and as the Indians were in a hostile mood they advised him against making any effort to work the mine. Disregarding their warnings Crittenden departed for the mine. He was armed with a repeating rifle and a Colt revolver.

When several days had passed and he had not returned to the fort, soldiers were sent out and found the horse and saddle about 10 miles down the San Pedro. The horse was tied and was almost dead from thirst. There was no trace of Crittenden. Whether he reached the mine and was killed by the Apaches, or the victim of an accident, was never known. The fact that an old rusty rifle was found many years ago on the edge of the desert below the mountain where the mine is said to be located, and the finding of a rusty Colt revolver just recently in that vicinity, would seem to indicate that Crittenden either lost his way while looking for the mine or met with an accident and died from heat and thirst.

The Apaches never revealed their secret to another white man, and it is doubtful if any living Indian today knows the location of the lost Yuma gold ledge.

MAXIMILIAN'S GOLD

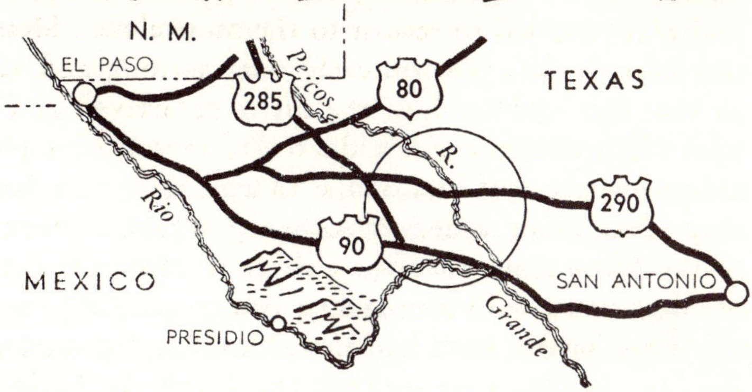

THERE IS A STORY told in Texas and many parts of Mexico that the puppet Emperor Maximilian, placed on the throne of Mexico by Napoleon III, early foresaw that the empire was doomed. In 1866, according to this legend, 15 heavily loaded carretas, closely covered with canvas and drawn by oxen, left Chapultepec castle in the dead of night and headed north. This was nearly a year before the empire fell and Maximilian was captured at Queretaro and executed with the Mexican traitors, Maramon and Mejia, at Cerro de las Campanas.

The caravan was in charge of four Austrians, close friends of the emperor, and guarded by 15 peons. After several forced marches, it reached Presidio del Norte and crossed to Texas soil. At that time the border between the United States and Mexico was the goal for many desperate men. Mexicans who had collaborated too freely with the French were fleeing to safety beyond the Rio Grande, while ex-Confederate soldiers and other Southerners, distrustful of their fate at the hands of carpet-baggers from the north, were crossing into Mexico.

At Presidio del Norte, the caravan met six ex-Confederate soldiers from Missouri, who had ridden west over the Chihuahua trail from San Antonio. The Austrian in charge of the caravan inquired anxiously concerning the condition of the road. He volunteered the information that he had a valuable cargo of flour that he must deliver in San Antonio. When informed by the Missourians that the road was strewn with the bones of animals and dead men, and that every mile of it was infested with bandits and hostile Indians, he seemed greatly disturbed. He offered to reward the Missourians handsomely if they would turn about and help guard the caravan across the plains to San Antonio.

The Missourians, glad to avail themselves of the opportunity to replenish their rapidly dwindling funds, agreed. When the men and jaded animals had refreshed themselves the caravan pulled out from Presidio del Norte with the six Missourians as scouts and outriders.

Everything went well for the first few days until the ex-Confederates had their curiosity aroused by the close manner in which the carts were guarded by the Austrians and peons. They were nearing the Pecos river when they decided to find out for themselves what the carts contained. They chose one of their number to make an investigation and report his findings. When the opportunity came the Missourian raised the canvas on several of the carts and was astounded to find they were loaded, not with flour, but with gold coin, gold and silver plate and chests of jewels. The ex-Confederates decided to kill the Austrians and the 15 peons and obtain the great treasure for themselves. At Castle Gap, 15 miles east of Horse Head crossing on the Pecos, the four Austrians and 15 peons were sound asleep after a hard day's march when the Missourians fell upon them and killed them.

After a hurried consultation the Missourians decided it would be unsafe to venture out on the plains with such a large treasure and only six men guarding it. They determined to take the gold needed for their immediate expenses, bury the rest and return for it when conditions were more peaceful. They dug a deep hole in the sand and dumped in the 15 cart-loads of money, gold and silver plate and the chests of jewels. The hole was partly filled with sand and the dead bodies of the four Austrians and 15 peons thrown into it. Then the carts, harness, and canvas were piled in and the whole set on fire, so the burial resembled nothing more than a burned out camp fire. The Mexican oxen were turned loose to shift for themselves in the marshes around the lake.

With their saddle bags bulging with gold coin, the six Missourians retraced their steps toward San Antonio to seek help of friends in recovering the treasure. One became ill and dropped out, agreeing to meet the others in San Antonio when he was able to travel. When he had recovered sufficiently to travel he came upon the mutilated bodies of his friends who had been killed and robbed of their ill-gotten gold.

The massacre left the one survivor sole owner of the great treasure. His horse was jaded and he was a sick man. However, he plodded on, evading Indians and bandits until he camped, by accident, with a band of horse thieves. During the night a sheriff and posse swooped down upon them and the Missourian was thrown in jail with the horse thieves. He was seriously ill and secured the services of a doctor. The town lawyer was called in and finally secured his release from jail. But the doctor told him that his malady was incurable and that he had only a few weeks or months to live.

Before dying the Missourian made a rough map to his treasure, which was useless to him now, and gave it to the lawyer and doctor. Many years later when the Indians had been rounded up and placed on reservations and the bandits were in jail or their graves, these two men took the map and went to Castle Gap to search for the treasure. The lake had gone dry and wind-blown sand had changed the topography of the country. It was impossible to locate any of the points called for in the map or waybill the ex-Confederate soldier had given them many long years before.

As far as this writer knows, that was the only effort ever made to locate Maximilian's great treasure at Castle Gap, 15 miles east of Horse Head crossing on the Pecos.

FROM A HIGH PASS in the Agua Dulce mountains, Padre Miguel Diaz and his Indian guides looked down upon the green vale of the Sonoyta. From the foot of a mountain gushed a crystal stream that flowed for many miles across the plain before sinking into the parched desert sands. Deer and antelope grazed on the grassy plains or rested in the shade of the trees that grew along the banks of the stream. Perched high on top of the Ajo mountains to the east, Montezuma peak stood silent guard over the upland plains.

So favorably impressed was Padre Diaz with the beautiful valley that he at once decided to build a mission there. After spending the night at Sonoyta the little party hurried back across the desert to St. George's bay where the clipper ship in which the padre had sailed from Spain rode at anchor. Supplies were unloaded on the beach and then packed on the backs of Indians to Sonoyta. When all was in readiness many Papago Indians were employed to make the adobes and dig the trenches for the rock foundation of the church.

The Papagos living in the vicinity were anxious to do the work. Day by day and week by week the walls grew higher and then after many months of hard work the church stood completed. Adjacent to the church in the center of a hollow square they erected a residence for the padre. Surrounding this was an arched cloister, forming a shady walk around the whole enclosure, and to the east was the garden, enclosing about five acres. All the buildings were surrounded by a high wall for protection against the Apaches. Farther south and fronting the mission was laid out a large square plaza surrounded by peon houses, a very orderly village.

The large church and all the buildings were painted white and presented a beautiful sight when viewed from the surrounding hills. The Papagos in all their lives had never seen anything like it. An *acequia* brought water from the river for the bathing place and the washing vats. When all this had been completed the garden was planted with seeds that the padre had brought from Spain. The Indians were already growing watermelons, squashes, chili peppers, corn and beans on their little farms along the river bank.

Horses and mules and some cattle were brought in from the older missions and rancherias along the Santa Cruz and San Pedro rivers. Prospecting parties were sent out and discovered rich quartz veins and deposits of placer gold in the San Francisco mountains only a few leagues south of the village. An adobe smelter was built near the church and many men were put to work washing the gravel and mining the rich quartz deposits. As fast as the ore was brought in it was smelted into gold bars. The nuggets and dust from the placer operations were put in strong buckskin bags. All the bars and bags were then placed in a secret underground room that had been constructed beneath the mission floor.

All the work of the mission was done by the Indians. Young girls cooked and waited table and looked after the rooms. Older women looked after the garden and the fruit trees and grapevines that grew in great profusion in the rich soil. Pomegranates, peaches, figs and many other kinds of fruit ripened in the warm sunshine of the little valley.

The Indians loved the beautiful mission which nestled like a jewel in the green valley surrounded on all sides by high mountains. But, as the years passed, they began to tire of the white man's life. The men complained of the long hours they had to work in the mines, the vineyards and the fields; the women and girls of the time they had to spend at the metates, grinding corn and wheat to make tortillas for the hungry miners and farmers. They longed for the carefree days before the black-robed fathers had come.

So, while the padre spread the gospel, the Papago neophytes planned revolution.

It was on a bright spring morning in the year 1750 when the sweet toned bells on the mission rang out over the little valley and the upland plains calling neophytes to early morning prayer. The sun was just tinting the eastern horizon and the air was sweet with the perfume from peach blossoms, when small groups of Indian men could be seen coming across the alley toward the church. Although it was a warm morning, all the Indians wore long blankets over their shoulders. The Indian women did not come to church that morning.

When the church was full of warriors, the chief and all the headmen drew large tomahawks from under their blankets and attacked Padre Diaz and the two visiting priests from Altar mission who happened to be spending a few days at Sonoyta. The bodies of the three dead priests were thrown into the underground rooms with the gold, and the walls and roof of the church were torn down. This massacre at Sonoyta started the uprising in which the missionaries at Caborca were killed and Bac and Guevavi were plundered and abandoned.

The entrance to the rich gold mine which was known as the Santa Lucia was covered over with large logs and earth and to this day has never been found. Old "Doctor Juan" a Papago Indian who died some years ago at the age of 128 years, confessed on his deathbed at Quitobaquita, that when just a small boy he was in the habit of playing around the ruins of the Sonoyta mission. One day just after a very hard rain he observed what at first seemed to be a slab of cement with a ring in it. Removing the dirt around the edges he gave it a tug and found that it covered a stairway leading down to an underground room. Entering this he found in one corner a large stack of gold bars. On top of the bars were a great number of old buckskin sacks filled with nuggets of placer gold. Some of the sacks had rotted, allowing the contents to trickle down and form golden piles on the stone floor of the little room. Upon seeing the three grinning skulls and piles of human bones in the other end of the room he became frightened and rushed out and replaced the slab of cement over the entrance. For more than a hundred years he kept the secret from Indian and white man alike.

In damp rainy weather strange lights flicker around the ancient ruins of Sonoyta, and the Papagos refuse to go near the mission site. Indians and many old Mexicans believe that wherever these ghostly white shimmering lights appear treasure is sure to be found.

Some years ago a party of Papagos was caught in a heavy rainstorm while out gathering fruit from the giant Saguaro cactus. The Indians were forced to take shelter near the old mission. As they huddled together in the dark for protection against the raging elements, the weird light appeared within the fallen walls. The women and old men refused to go near it and cautioned the younger men about doing so. However, one young Indian who had been away to school laughed at the idea of a ghost being able to hurt anyone. Despite his elders' warning he sharpened a stick and hurried over to drive it in the spot where the weird shimmering light was rising and falling. After driving the stake in the ground he rose to go but something held him fast and he could not move. He fainted from fright, and it took the combined strength of two husky companions to rescue him.

The Papago medicine man tried for two days to drive away the spook that would harm one of their young men, before it was finally discovered that in driving the stake to mark the spot, the young buck had driven it through the lower end of one of his pant legs pinning himself firmly to the ground.

In any event, the Papagos never ventured back to Sonoyta. The big pile of gold bars presumably still is there, and the nuggets and dust in the rotted buckskin sacks are still trickling down and forming piles of placer gold on the cobblestone floor of the little underground room beneath the floor of the old mission at Sonoyta.

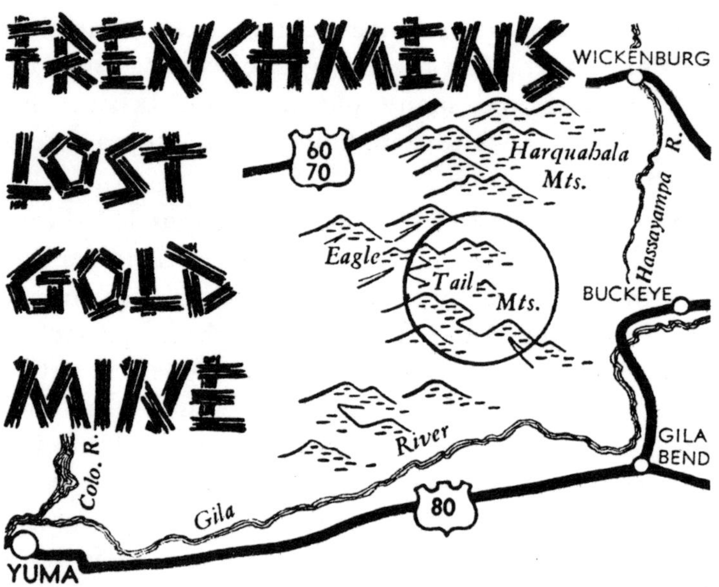

THERE WAS CONSIDERABLE excitement in the little frontier town of Yuma in the spring of 1867 when two Frenchmen halted their pack outfit in front of the W. B. Hooper and company store. From one of their pack mules they unloaded a large amount of rough gold that had been hammered from rusty looking quartz, bits of which still clung to some of the larger pieces of gold.

After purchasing additional mules and supplies the two men still had $8,000 on deposit to their credit in the Hooper store. After spending several days in town the men headed their pack train out into the desert in the direction of the Eagle Tail mountains. Many of the male inhabitants of Yuma set out to follow the prospectors into the hills, but lost track of them the first night out.

The two men were never seen alive again and nothing was ever heard of them. The $8,000 was still on deposit at the Hooper store 20 years later. Some years later two skeletons were discovered in the mountains to the east, but there was no way of identifying them. Many oldtimers believe that those piles of bleaching bones were all that was left of the two Frenchmen.

In 1873, King Woolsey and his men were out chasing Apache Indians for the bounty money their scalps would bring. One day when riding a well marked trail through the Tenhachape pass they came upon a large pile of rich gold ore. Some years later an expedition was sent out to locate and

There was considerable excitement in the little frontier town of Yuma when two Frenchmen halted their pack outfit and from one of the mules unloaded a large amount of rough gold.

remove the ore. The ore was taken to Yuma, but the mine from which it had been taken could not be found.

Lincoln Fowler and a brother prospecting in the Harquahala country in 1889 discovered an old working on a gold ledge and the remains of a camp nearby. There was nothing to indicate when or by whom it had been worked. Closer examination proved the outcrop to have been a rich pocket, but only a few small pieces of the ore were found scattered about.

A. H. Peeples of La Paz and Rich Hill fame once stated that in 1868 while passing through the Harquahala country he came upon three Frenchmen who were working a prospect nearby their camp and seemed to be doing well. However, on the return trip to Yuma, Peeples found the camp burned and the skeleton of what seemed to be a white man. Some Maricopa Indians were then in the vicinity and were believed to have been responsible for the killing.

Experienced miners of that time pointed out that it was very unlikely that the two Frenchmen would have packed their ore all the way from the Harquahala country to the Tenhachape pass when it would have been much easier for them to have taken it to the Hassayampa river and ground it in arrastres.

Many of the old time prospectors and desert rats around Yuma have looked for the rich outcropping from which the two Frenchmen took their ore. Most of the searching has been done in the Tenhachape pass country where the pile of rich ore was found by Woolsey and his men.

The firm of W. B. Hooper and company was later changed to Hooper, Barney and company, but is now out of business.

The late George Sears of Ajo and Gunsight vowed there was plenty of gold in the Eagle Tail mountains—and George had about 25 pounds of rusty looking gold quartz to prove it. Sears was on his way from Phoenix to Ajo one time and decided to detour west and prospect the Eagle Tail mountains. He carried with him on his pack animals a small roll of bedding and grub.

He spent the night after a hard rain near a small depression on the side of a wash in the Eagle Tails and the next morning while getting breakfast noticed his hobbled jacks drinking water from what looked like a shallow prospect hole. There were some loose rocks on the small dump below the hole. After breakfast he packed up and when passing by the hole filled his canteen and threw some of the rusty looking pieces of rock into the pack box with his grip to balance the load more evenly.

As his food supply diminished he found it necessary to balance his load several times by picking up rocks along the way. When George finally reached the Gunsight mine 16 miles east of Ajo there was not much food left in the grub box, but in unloading the pack box he discovered that the rocks he had put in first in the Eagle Tail mountains were chock full of free gold. Sears was never quite sure whether he could find the place where he picked up the golden rocks that morning, but he had the rocks to prove to any doubting Thomas that there is gold in the Eagle Tails.

Whether the shallow hole from which old George Sears took the rusty chunks of rich gold quartz has any connection with the Lost Frenchman mine would be difficult to say. However, the ore found by Sears seemed to be the same kind from which the Frenchmen pounded their $8,000 worth of gold and is said to be the same kind of ore that was found by King Woolsey and his men in the Tenhachape pass country.

LOST BREYFOGLE MINE

IN THE EARLY SPRING of 1863, three prospectors, Breyfogle, O'Bannion and McLeod, stopped at the Las Vegas ranch in southern Nevada. After refreshing themselves for a few days at the cool springs in the shade of the great cottonwoods, the three partners started out across the burning sands to the south.

Several weeks later Breyfogle returned alone. He was in an exhausted condition for want of water and was suffering from a fractured skull. In a red bandana handkerchief he carried several pounds of rich gold ore. When his wound had been dressed and he had been given food and drink he told this story:

Three days after leaving the ranch he and his partners established camp at a small spring high up on the side of a mountain range at the end of a narrow box canyon. One day three Pahute Indians came into camp and told of a rich gold ledge about three miles away.

Breyfogle went with the Indians to see the mine and get samples of the ore. On the way back an Indian walking behind Breyfogle felled him with a tomahawk blow on the head and left him for dead. Breyfogle regained consciousness during the night and made his way back to camp where he found his two partners murdered. Their small supply of provisions and their firearms were gone.

Breyfogle, in a dazed condition and suffering greatly from his fractured skull, made his way back across the desert to the Vegas ranch arriving there three days later. When he was well enough to travel he again headed out across the great desert in the direction of Austin, Nevada, where he organized several expeditions to search for the little spring and the wonderful outcropping of pink quartz. He was never quite right in the head after being struck down by the Indian and was unable to locate any place that even looked like the one shown him by the three Pahutes.

There are several versions of the story, but the most likely places the ledge in the McCullough mountains a few miles north of Crescent, Nevada. The writer stopped at the Vegas ranch many years ago and was given two small pieces of the ore left there by Breyfogle, and at a small spring high up on the west side of the McCullough mountains he found the ruins of a deserted camp including some badly rusted cooking utensils. In a crevice above the fireplace at the base of a perpendicular rock was found about ten pounds of the same kind of ore that Breyfogle had left at the Vegas ranch. The dim trail led out from the spring toward the northeast.

The vein has never been relocated since Breyfogle left. The samples found in the crevice above the old fireplace assayed $6,780 per ton in gold.

LOST GLORIA PAN

LLUVIA DE ORO and the Gloria Pan were two of the richest mines ever discovered in Mexico—the Lluvia de Oro in recent times and the Gloria Pan in the days of the padres.

About 40 years ago, a Sinaloa Indian rode out from his mountain home to a nearby village where the fiesta of San Juan was being celebrated. After having danced the deer and snake dances all night and partaking freely of liquid refreshments, he lay down on his serape for a little nap.

Soon another peon happened along and overheard the Sinaloan talking in his sleep about two rich mines he had discovered in the mountains near his home. The peon hurried home and told his patron what he had overheard. Several days later the Indian was induced to show one of his mines, and shortly thereafter it proved to be one of the richest gold mines ever discovered in Mexico. Because of the great abundance of free gold in the rock, it was called the Lluvia de Oro, "Shower of Gold."

In return for showing this great mine, the poor Indian was given only the meat of an old bull, the stingy patron keeping the hide for himself. Disappointed at the treatment he had received, the Indian refused to show the Gloria Pan to anyone and died some years later taking the secret with him to his grave.

The Gloria Pan was discovered in 1750 and was being operated by the Jesuits in 1767 when the Spanish king, Charles III issued the edict that all Jesuits should be expelled from Spain and its possessions. For 17 years the gold from one of the richest mines in Mexico had piled up. There is little doubt that the Jesuits had foreseen that they would not be able to take any of their treasure out of the country and that it would possibly be confiscated, for their records brought over from Spain in recent years show that a large number of Indians were employed in carrying the treasure up the mountain and storing it in the mine. When the mine was sealed up it contained several million dollars in gold bars in addition to large bodies of rich gold ore ready to be mined. The Jesuits, unable to take any of their treasure out of the country, left without it, never to return.

Every year prospectors search the brush-covered hills for the wonderful mine and its great treasure, but no trace of it has ever been found. There are other Indians, it is believed, who could reveal the hiding place; but, remembering the treatment received by their countryman after showing the Lluvia de Oro, they refuse to guide anyone to the Gloria Pan.

The niggardly patron had bought the Lluvia de Oro for

next to nothing. But, by mistreating the Indian who had showed him the rich mine, he had lost a chance to add millions of dollars more to his wealth.

LOST TREASURE OF CARRETA CANYON

A PIECE OF SILVER ORE assaying thousands of ounces per ton recently discovered in an old adobe house that stands on the main street in the old pueblo of Arivaca in southern Arizona may be the clue that eventually will lead to the discovery of a long lost, fabulously rich silver mine and a great treasure said to be stored away in the tunnel.

According to stories told by some of the descendents of the Spanish Conquistadores who still reside in and around *el Pueblo de Arivaca,* the mine is located somewhere along the old carreta road that ran from the ancient Tumacacori mission on the west bank of the Santa Cruz river below Tubac to Sonoyta, south of the present mining town of Ajo, Arizona.

Don Manuel Gonzales, who arrived in Arivaca in the early '80s, before the wild Apaches had been rounded up by the joint action of the American and Mexican governments and placed on reservations, vouches for the authenticity of the story.

It was siesta-time in the old pueblo and all along Arivaca creek, and I found Don Manuel asleep in the noon-day sun. Far across the Altar valley to the northwest a fleecy cloud hung like a bridal veil from the lofty summit of Baboquivari peak, the highest in southern Arizona.

Don Manuel bade me be seated and after proffering the inevitable *cafecita,* this fine old Mexican gentleman, in accordance with a custom that lingers among polite Spanish-Americans, gave me his house and garden and all that he possessed. Don Manuel lit a cigarette, offered one to me and sat looking at the lighted match, seemingly lost in deep thought.

Finally, when the rings of smoke started drifting up over the cool veranda on which we sat, he came to with a start and asked me if I had ever heard the story of the old carreta and the lost silver mine at the upper end of Carreta canyon. I assured him that while I had read many of the old records and accounts of the numerous mines worked by the Jesuits from the Tumacacori mission, I had not heard the one referred to at first hand.

"Well," said Don Manuel, "shortly after my arrival in the Arivaca country, three Mexican vaqueros started out to round up cattle that grazed on the western foothills of the Tumacacori and Tascosa mountains. The boys established their camp and left their chuck wagon on the plains near the mouth of Jalisco canyon only a few miles east of *el Pueblo de Arivaca.*

"After arranging their camp the three vaqueros started off in different directions to gather the cattle and drive them to the corral where they were to be branded. The vaquero who rode south soon found himself near the head of a long rocky canyon on the western slopes of the rugged Tascosa range and not far from the pass that leads to the deep canyons that gash the south side of this range.

"As he stood there surveying the surrounding country that spread out below him he discovered his horse was standing on an old mine dump and that off to one side was the entrance to a tunnel that had a heavy oaken door with a handmade hasp and staple on which was fastened a large padlock such as was used by the Spaniards and old time Mexicans. From a large pile of ore that lay on the dump in front of the tunnel the vaquero selected a few pieces to take with him and rode on after the racing cattle that were heading down the canyon to the valley below. A short distance below the tunnel on one side of the canyon stood the remains of an old carreta such as was used by the padres during the Spanish occupation.

"That night as they sat around the campfire at the chuck wagon eating their evening meal, the vaquero displayed his samples of ore and told the others that he had discovered an old tunnel with a wooden door fastened with a large padlock. When the other boys started to ridicule him about his lost mine, he said no more about it, but when the roundup was over he took the pieces of silver ore home with him and left them in the old adobe house where one of them was found and is now in the possession of a man living in Casa Grande, Arizona.

"The vaquero drifted away to another part of the country. Nothing more was heard of the old tunnel until a few years later when a party of Spaniards arrived in the district from San Francisco, with an old Spanish document describing a long lost and fabulously rich silver mine in which was stored a part of the Tumacacori treasure that had been hidden by a Jesuit priest from the Tumacacori mission.

"One of the guide posts to the mine," continued Don Manuel, "was an old carreta that had been abandoned near the tunnel. At that time no one in Arivaca had ever heard of the old ox cart, and as the only man who knew anything about the old tunnel had disappeared, the Spaniards returned empty handed to San Francisco."

In the spring of 1886 soldiers chasing Apaches who had raided the Peck ranch in Peck canyon, killing the owner and his wife and leaving their baby boy Al alive in the cabin, passed by the old carreta high up near the head of a long canyon which since has been named "Carreta canyon." At that time the soldiers had never heard the story of the long lost silver mine and treasure and were too busy chasing Apache renegades to do any prospecting.

Calistro, an Opata Indian who was born and raised near the Tumacacori mission, once repeated to the writer the story told to him by his father and grandfather. They said that when the Pima tribes revolted against their Spanish oppressors and started the great uprising in 1750, the padre in charge of the mines and mission decided to conceal the entrance to the mines, bury their treasure and flee to the coast.

According to Calistro's story, the padre chose a few of the loyal neophytes to help him load all the altar fixtures, many bars of gold and silver bullion, a small copper box containing the maps of the eight mines and church records, into a carreta which was drawn by two oxen.

At dawn the padre left the mission. An Indian on foot prodded the slow oxen over the old road that leads out across the rocky foothills and around the north end of the Tumacacori mountains past the Isabella mine where the road may still be seen cut in the solid rock on the hillside just west of the Isabella shaft and ruins of an old rock house. From the Isabella mine they skirted the foothills below the San Pedro mine and wound their way through the mesquite into the foothills of the rugged Tascosa mountains where they were met by a pack train from the Altar mission in Sonora. The padre in charge of the pack train informed them that the Indians at Altar had revolted and killed a number of Spaniards and that conditions were very bad there.

While the two padres were holding a conference, word reached them by Indian runners that the revolt was widespread and that three padres had been killed at Sonoyta and their bodies thrown in an underground room with the treasure, and the walls of the mission pulled down. In view of the serious situation that was developing, it was decided to bury the cartload from Tumacacori and the eight pack mule loads of treasure from the Altar mission in the tunnel at the nearby silver mine until such time as they could return in safety for it.

After concealing their treasure and abandoning their carreta and six of the mules, the padres made their way to the coast and the ships that were to carry them away. In 1767 King Charles III issued the edict that expelled the Jesuit order from Spain and all its possessions, and they were never able to return for their treasures.

The contents of the old carreta from Tumacacori and the eight jack loads of treasure from the Altar mission are still stored away in the old tunnel up there in the hills near the head of Carreta canyon, guarded by the skeleton of the old Opata who prodded the slow oxen over the rocky road across the foothills to the mouth of the tunnel. The copper box has a screw in one corner. Remove the screw, pull out the iron bar and open the box. There will be found all the maps of the eight mines that belonged to Tumacacori and the great treasure stored away in them.

LOST PESH-LA-CHI

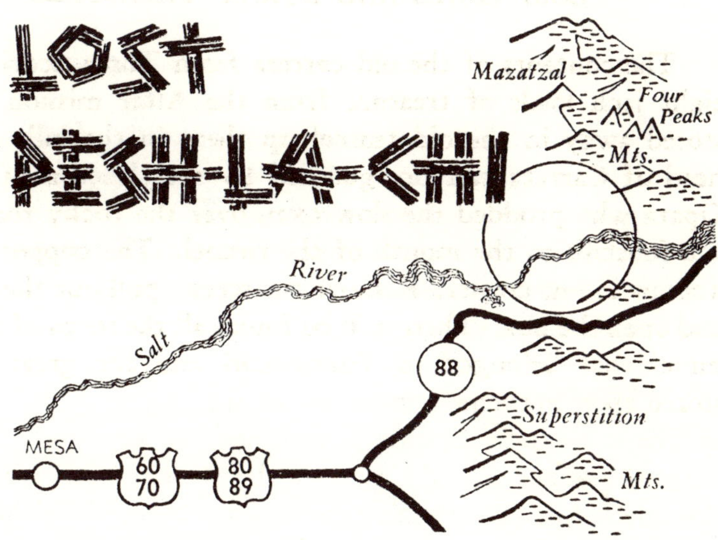

DOCTOR THORNE, an Arizona pioneer, spent the last 39 years of a long and eventful life in and around the rugged ravines of the Four Peaks country, northeast of the city of Phoenix, Arizona, searching for a fabulously rich gold ledge said to have been shown to him by the Tonto Apache Indians during the many years that he was held a prisoner by the tribe.

It was in 1849 that Thorne, then a young physician just out of school, set out across the great plains infested with hostile Indians. A year later he was captured by the Tonto Apaches. The Indians treated him well but, recognizing his skill as a physician, refused to turn him loose.

In the year 1861, about the time the Civil war broke out, a great drouth came upon the Indian country. Pinyon nuts and seeds of all kinds were scarce, and wild game drifted away in search of feed. The Apache warriors were all out raiding and to make things worse disease broke out among the women and children of the tribe.

The Indians believed that certain kinds of diseases were caused by different kinds of animals. If caused by a snake, the medicine man danced the snake dance to the accompaniment of weird music made by a gourd filled with pebbles. If the disease was thought to be caused by a deer, the medicine man decked himself in a headdress adorned with deer horns and danced the deer dance.

When the Apache medicine man had exhausted his hatful of tricks without finding a cure and the epidemic continued to grow worse, the old men of the tribe appealed to Doctor Thorne for help. Realizing the seriousness of the situation and that his reputation as a physician was at stake, Thorne decided to use one of his strongest remedies—hickemia, a tuber that still grows profusely over many parts of Arizona.

How the Creator of all things managed to wrap up so much dynamite in such a harmless looking little root is beyond the power of science to determine. One teaspoon of the powder made from it was sufficient to stir the vitals of a drugstore Indian. But the remedy worked like magic, and Doctor Thorne tapered off the cure with a gourdful of soothing squaw tea, made from a bush found all over the west. By tom-tom, smoke signal and grapevine telegraph, the doctor's fame spread far beyond the borders of Apacheland.

Indians, like elephants, never forget. So when the warriors returned from their raids, a powwow was held, and it was decided to release the doctor in order that he might return to his own people. To show their gratitude they agreed to show him their gold mine, Pesh-la-chi.

On the day set for release they placed Thorne on a horse

On the day set for his release, they placed Thorne on a horse and headed out of the mountains.

and with six feathered warriors as an escort the little party headed out of the mountains in a southerly direction. After riding the skyline of several high ridges they dropped down into the lower country and skirted a high mountain to the northeast of the Superstitions. Late in the afternoon a stop was made and a blindfold was placed over the doctor's eyes.

Just before sundown the three warriors who were riding ahead halted and asked Thorne to dismount. When the others came up the blindfold was removed and Thorne found himself standing in a narrow canyon. When his eyes had become accustomed to the sunlight, he saw at his feet a white quartz vein about 18 inches wide, cutting across the bed of the canyon and outcropping in the walls on each side. The vein was full of bright yellow metal that glistened in the sunlight. Before the blindfold was replaced Thorne looked up and saw the Four Peaks vividly outlined against the sky. The sun was at his back, so the vein must have been either on the south or west side of the Four Peaks mountains.

As the party rode down the sunset trail the doctor tried to remember the landmarks so he could return later and work the mine, reimbursing himself for the long years that he had been held in captivity.

Early the following morning Thorne was released on the edge of the desert east of what is now the city of Phoenix. Years later when the Apaches had been rounded up and placed on reservations, Thorne returned to the desert country and started the long search for the white quartz vein.

He made many trips into the Four Peaks country and was well known to a number of old timers living in Tempe and Mesa. To these friends he talked freely of his mine and of his experiences among the Tonto Apaches during the years that he had lived with them. When too old and feeble to endure the many hardships of the rugged mountains he went to the Rio Grande country in New Mexico, where he died without having found a place that resembled the canyon where the Indians had showed him the wonderful vein of gold ore in the days of his youth.

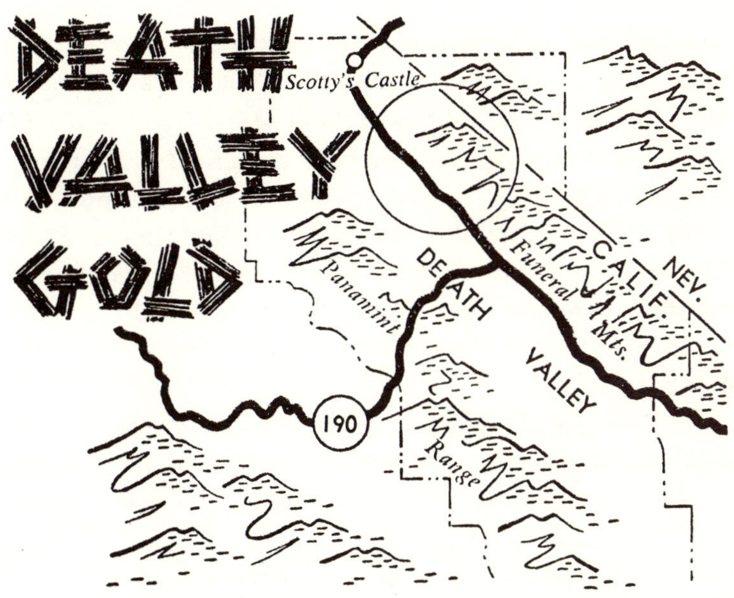

HIGH UP ALONG the eastern edge of Death Valley and not many hours' journey from Scotty's castle, there was discovered one of the richest deposits of placer gold ever found on the American continent.

Incredible as it may seem, 500 emigrants on their way from southern Utah to the new gold fields of California in '49 and '50, passed over, and many of them died within sight of what may prove to be the El Dorado of the great Southwest.

According to the story, two Pahute Indian brothers, many years ago, trudging along over the hot sand on the western edge of a dry lake searching for horses that had strayed from their camp, saw in the distance what appeared to be the entrance to an abandoned tunnel. Further investigation proved it to be the mouth of a cave. The overhanging rocks formed a cool shelter offering protection from the fierce rays of the summer sun, and the brothers were glad to avail themselves of the opportunity to rest in the shade.

A cool breeze came from the depths of the cave, and they heard the sound of running water in the distance. Removing pieces of limestone that had fallen from the roof and partly blocked the entrance, they went along the narrow tunnel to a point where the floor sloped downward and the walls opened out into a large dome-shaped cavern with a dark pool of water at the bottom.

Water boiled up from the center of the pool and formed waves that dashed against the rocky shore and broke into fine spray. The shore of the lake resembled a great amphitheatre with step-like terraces extending down to the water's edge. The water bubbled up from the subterranean depths with such great force that it brought great amounts of heavy black sand and piled them on the terraces around the lake. Some of the sand trickled back into the pool only to be brought up again and again.

One of the Pahutes took a handful of this sand out into the sunlight. It sparkled with small nuggets and flakes of gold, all worn smooth from constant churning in the pool. Returning to the cave again, the Indians were surprised to see that the water was receding, leaving thousands of tons of the rich sand stranded on the terraces around the edge of the lake. It was growing late in the evening when the brothers made their way back to camp.

Keeping their secret to themselves, they left early in the morning, taking with them a wagon and several sacks. Entering the cave again they found it full of water just as it had been the previous day. The small waves were rolling and breaking against the shores as if in some mysterious way they were connected with the tides in the Pacific ocean.

After filling their sacks with the golden sands the two brothers decided to explore the cave. By the dim light of a primitive torch they had brought along, they could see hanging from the dome-shaped roof long beautifully colored crystals resembling great icicles. Stalagmites stood up encrusted all over with gems that sparkled like diamonds. Here before their eyes beneath the burning desert sands was a magic castle that out-rivaled a chapter from the Arabian Nights. Here in this Aladdin's cave strewn about on the floor and in the dark pool lay thousands—perhaps millions of dollars worth of gold. Never in all their lives had they seen anything like it.

Near the center of the pool was a small rocky island. One of the brothers decided to swim to it. When he had reached a point about half way across, the bottom seemed to drop out of the pool and the water rushed into the subterranean outlet with a gurgling roar, taking the unfortunate Indian down with it. The other Indian remained for several days and although the water in the pool continued to rise and fall with the tide, he never saw his brother again.

Among many Indian tribes there is a taboo against returning to the place where one of their number has met death. So the Pahute never again saw the gold cavern beneath the burning sands of *To-me-sha.*

Ancient water lines around the dry lake bed below the cave indicate that in prehistoric times when the water level in the Pacific ocean was higher than today, the lake may have been filled with water from some subterranean source—just as the pool in the cave was filled when the Pahutes found it. The bedrock of the dry lake is known to be covered with several feet of black sand which from all indications was forced out of the cave with the water. The gold presumably settled to the bottom upon entering the quiet water of the lake.

It is a fact that there are several of these caverns in Death Valley from which water apparently gushed in ancient times. Perhaps some of them contain black sand and gold like the one herein described. It has even been suggested that the gold-laden sands of such a cavern may be the source of the mysterious wealth of Death Valley Scotty.

LOST SOAPMAKER MINE

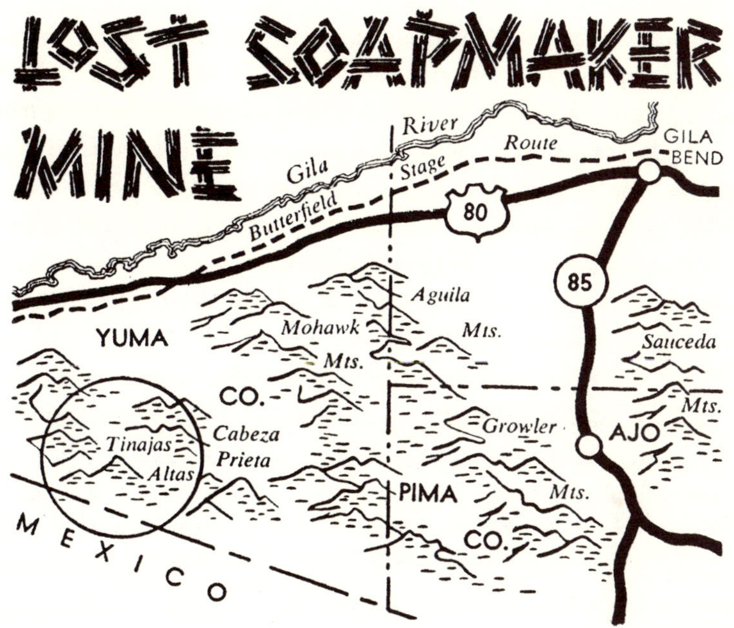

IN THE YEAR 1850 a small party of Mexicans on their way to California from the little town of Caborca, in the state of Sonora, Mexico, passed through what is now the southwest part of Pima county, Arizona. They were headed for a crossing on the Colorado river near the present city of Yuma, where they hoped to strike a trail that was afterward known as the Butterfield stage route to California.

They camped one night near Tinajas Altas, 70 or 80 miles west of the present mining town of Ajo, Arizona. Some of the pack animals strayed off during the night; the next morning, while looking for them, a Mexican climbed up the side of a small round mountain in order to get a better view of the surrounding country and if possible locate the missing animals. He had gone only a short distance when his attention was attracted to a very rich vein of gold ore protruding through the white sand that was piled up on the south side of the mountain. Further investigation revealed a vein about two feet wide very rich in gold. There was a streak of strawberry colored quartz about seven or eight inches wide running along the hangingwall side of the vein that was literally matted together with wire and coarse gold.

Before returning to camp with the animals the Mexican noted the surroundings to make sure that he could return again and find the vein. He discovered that the vein was slowly being covered by drifting sand that the south wind blew up daily from the desert below. To the west from where he stood he could see Cabeza Prieta (Black Head) mountain vividly outlined against the sky. The mountain on which he stood was small and round and the vein was about one-third of the way up the south side and was running in a northwesterly-southeasterly direction. After selecting a few samples of the ore he returned to camp with the missing animals and shortly thereafter returned to Caborca in order to get help to return and work the mine. A German soapmaker at Caborca was interested in the venture and was soon on his way to the mine with the discoverer, two other Mexicans and a pack outfit loaded with provisions and tools to work the mine.

Upon reaching the country in which the mine was located they camped at a small spring some distance to the south and there built a small arrastre in which to grind the rich ore. They had no trouble in finding the vein and started immediate operations. They made several weekly trips to the mine and each time returned to camp with the pack animals loaded with rich ore. Then one day when they were all at the mine taking out ore, three young Papago Indians appeared at the top of the shallow shaft and shot them full of arrows before they could escape. After making sure that they were all dead, the Indians filled the hole with cactus and sand and, after robbing the camp, never returned.

Relatives of the murdered men made several trips from Caborca to the vicinity but were never able to locate the mine or get any trace of the three Mexicans or the soapmaker. When old "Doctor Juan," a Papago Indian medicine man, told the writer this story, he was 128 years old and was on his death bed at Quitobaquita, south of Ajo, Arizona. Old Juan was the sole survivor of the little band of Papagos that had killed the four miners 70 years before.

Very rich float has in years past been picked up by prospectors and cowboys riding the range in that part of the country. Hardly a year goes by that some expedition outfitted from Ajo or Yuma does not head into the desert wastes in search of this rich gold ledge. A million dollars in gold could quickly be taken from such a vein as the one described to the writer by old Doctor Juan, as he lay on his deathbed more than 37 years ago. Ore assaying $25,000 per ton in gold is worth looking for, even though it is located in the heart of a great desert.

This story of Tim Cody's
Lost Ledge was written
by Harold O. Weight

TIM CODY'S LOST LEDGE

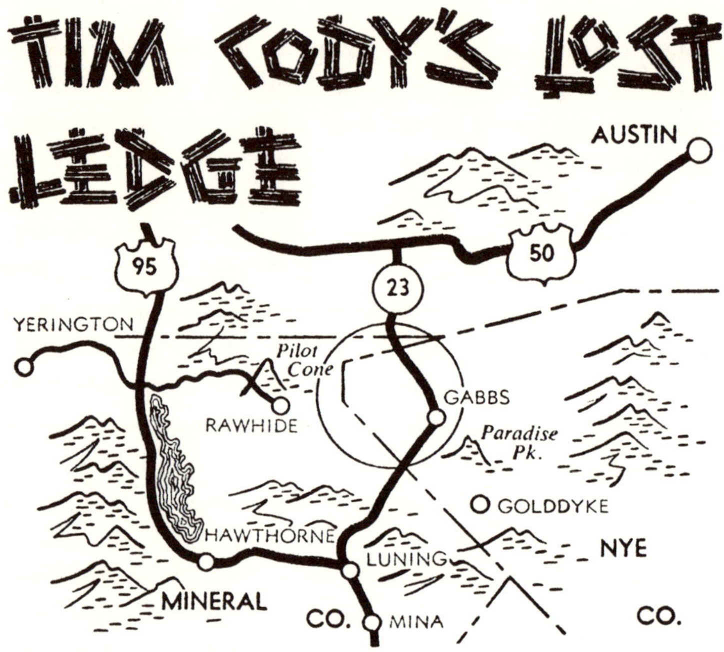

SOMEWHERE NEAR the base of Cedar mountain, which lies on the border between Nye and Mineral counties, Nevada, is a little knoll crowned with gnarled juniper or desert cedar. One of the junipers—if it still stands—shows cuts and scars where Tim Cody marked it nearly 40 years ago. And near the base of the marked juniper is a ledge of iron-stained white quartz spotted with the yellow shine of free gold. Tim stumbled on the ledge in 1908, then lost it and never was able to relocate it.

Tim Cody really should not have been a prospector, since he lacked one of the most important single qualifications for the job—a good sense of direction. Tim could lose himself easily even when sober—and he was not always sober. He was an old-country Irishman, good-hearted, friendly, but poorly educated and not always able to think a situation out. He was a big, rawboned man with sandy hair and complexion, about 40 years old, when he found and lost the only real strike of his prospecting career.

Tim may not have had the qualifications for prospecting, but he had a real love for the job. He worked willingly enough in the mines, but as soon as he earned enough for a supply of bacon and beans, he packed his outfit and headed for the hills. In 1908, he was camped at Stewart springs, about 20 miles northeast of Mina, prospecting the area which later became part of the Simon district.

One day he decided to walk from his camp to the mining town of Golddyke about 15 miles to the north, at the base of the Paradise range. Perhaps his food supply was running short or perhaps he felt the need of a sociable time with the boys. At any rate, he struck directly across country toward the mining camp. He carried only a small supply of water and no food, expecting to reach his destination in a few hours.

To reach Golddyke, Tim had to cross parts of an old lake bed which had been thoroughly eroded in the thousands of years that had elapsed since the lake had vanished. Somehow Tim became lost and wandered throughout the day. Toward nightfall he found himself at the foot of a knoll covered with junipers. Hoping to orient himself he climbed to the top of the knoll. Paradise peak, north and east of Golddyke, is the highest mountain in the area, and from the top of the knoll Tim saw and recognized it. And to the west he saw the black pyramid called Pilot Cone, which rises near Rawhide. The two peaks gave him his directions again, and with a sigh of relief, he sat down to rest.

"I lit my pipe," he said, "and looked down at my feet. There was a lot of white quartz stained with iron." Tim was a prospector. He picked up a piece of the quartz and broke it. The fresh surface was rich with free gold—gold that Tim could see with his naked eyes, even in the gathering dusk. He dropped to his knees and kept breaking the quartz which lay about him. Every piece contained gold. The Irishman knew that at last fortune was within his reach.

It was nearly dark, but Tim had gold fever. The thought of waiting until morning was unbearable. But he knew that he must mark the spot somehow so that he could find it again on his return. He took his prospecting pick and chopped savagely at the nearest juniper. He didn't think of burning some of the trees—or perhaps he was afraid that the fire would attract unwelcome investigators.

When he was certain that he could recognize the tree again, he loaded himself with all the ore he could carry and struck out again for Golddyke.

And then Tim got lost again. What happened, he never was able to explain. "I seemed to kind of go blind," he said. "I couldn't find my way."

He wandered dazedly for three days. Then he found himself at the abandoned Pactolus mine less than 10 miles from his starting point at Stewart springs. He still had pieces of the ore with him, but his only interest was in water and food. Normally there would have been no water at Pactolus but someone had left a supply in the old dugout at the mine. In the dugout Tim also found some flour. The rats had been in it, but he wolfed it down hungrily.

After resting, Tim went on to Golddyke, and reached the town without difficulty. From Golddyke he returned to his camp at Stewart springs, looking for the cedar-crowned knoll on the way. He did not find it. He had no idea of where his wanderings had taken him during the nearly 100 hours from the time he left Stewart springs until he found himself at Pactolus. All he knew was that somewhere in the area he had covered, among the many juniper-topped knolls was one from which you could see both Paradise peak and Pilot Cone, and that a fortune in gold was waiting for him on that knoll.

Tim was certain that he could find his vein again. He went into Mina and showed his specimens there—probably with the idea of obtaining a grubstake. He did finance himself in some fashion, and returned to Stewart springs and spent a full year searching for the knoll. He did not find it. Until his death in the early 1930s in the hospital at Hawthorne, Nevada, Tim talked about his lost ledge and hunted for it whenever the opportunity arose.

Men still alive in Mina saw the ore Tim Cody brought in. Many have tried to find it, to retrace the course Tim followed in those four days of wandering. They couldn't do it. But about 1915, Bill Robinson and Bert Whitney found a piece of float just over the summit of a little hill about three quarters of a mile from Stewart springs. It was white, iron-stained quartz rich in free gold. Try as they would, they could not locate its source. Perhaps they were close to Tim Cody's lost knoll—and perhaps it was a piece of ore that Tim had dropped in his wanderings.

Just before he died Tim told Carl E. Sullivan, now county commissioner of Mineral county: "I think all the time I was looking too low down." Perhaps he meant too low in the lake bed. Perhaps too far south.

Carl Sullivan knew Tim well. He brought Tim's body

back from Hawthorne and buried him in the cemetery at Mina.

"I liked the old fellow—liked him fine," Carl told me. "And I believe he really found the gold there—and I don't think it was more than two or three miles from Stewart springs. It's gold country out that way. Two gold mines, the Warrior and the Omco, operated near there. But neither is the vein that Tim lost—the gold isn't visible. It's so finely divided that if you get one color in a pan, the ore will run $15 a ton. You have to grind it to 200 mesh to save the values.

"No, Tim's gold is still out there—but there are just too many knolls with juniper on them."

LOST BLACK MAVERICK MINE

BACK OF MOST LOST MINE stories is a thread of truth. In telling and retelling, the mine usually becomes fabulously rich, and new details are added until the historical facts are completely lost or so distorted as to have little factual value.

An exception to this is the story of the Lost Maverick. There are many people living today who knew Yaqui Valentino, saw the rich specimen of ore he had and heard the story of discovery from his own lips. Among those who knew him are Mr. and Mrs. Henry Hardt of Chandler, Arizona.

Many years ago an Indian cowboy locally known as "Yaqui Valentino" was riding the range in the Four Peaks country northeast of Phoenix. One day he was chasing a two-year-old black maverick bull through the manzanita and scrub oak that grow profusely on the lower reaches of the Four Peaks, when he suddenly came out into a clearing through which trickled a small stream of water. As they entered the little clearing the loop of Valentino's 60-foot riata spun through the air and landed gracefully around the neck of the racing bull. The trained horse sat back on his haunches and the maverick turned a flip-flop in the air and landed on his back in a small puddle of clear water. In his struggles to regain his feet he scoured the sand off the richest specimen of gold ore the cowboy had ever seen.

When he had finished tying and marking the bull Valentino picked up the piece of ore and put it in his pocket. When he had released the maverick the cowboy saw that his horse was breaking through some rotten timbers into what seemed to be the workings of an old pit that had been covered over. As he led his horse away he saw the foundations of a cabin with a large tree growing up through the floor. Nearby the tree was a rusty pick such as was used by Spanish and Mexican miners hundreds of years ago. The pick had lain there so long there was little but the eye left. There was nothing to identify the former occupants of the abandoned camp.

After leaving the Four Peaks country Valentino rode for the Bar-T-Bar outfit at Rye where many of the old time cowmen and miners saw the piece of rich ore and heard Valentino tell the story of how he found it. It is said that one old-timer, angered at his failure to get the Indian to show him the mine, suggested to the cowhands that they force him to take them to it and then shoot the Yaqui and throw him off of one of the high bluffs into the canyon. A Mexican cowboy happened to overhear the conversation and notified the Yaqui.

Two men came in one day and reported that they had

In his struggles to regain his feet the maverick scoured the sand off of the richest specimen of gold ore the cowboy had ever seen.

found the remains of an old camp and believed it to be the same one the Indian described. The Yaqui was angry at first. But when he was told the location of the new find he threw his hat into the air and shouted that it could not be his mine as it was located many miles away from where he had found the old camp and the piece of rich ore.

Among the Yaqui's friends were Mr. and Mrs. Henry Hardt. He liked them very much and wanted them to share in his good fortune by helping him locate and develop the mine. After much talk it was decided that each should have a one-third interest in the mine and it would henceforth be known as the "Black Maverick."

The trip to the Four Peaks country had been planned and

excitement was running high when Valentino came into camp and told Mrs. Hardt that he had had a very bad dream the night before in which he had seen a large number of Apache Indians shooting at him from the top of a hill near his mine. The Indian was badly disturbed as he had been taught during his childhood days in Sonora that to disclose the location of a lost mine to anyone outside of the tribe meant instant death at the hands of the Yaqui gods.

After Mrs. Hardt had explained that his fears were based on superstition and that he would not be harmed in any way, the party set forth from Payson for the Four Peaks country. The Indian seemed nervous and ill at ease. Two days later when they had reached a point on the western foothills directly opposite the four lofty peaks, the Yaqui became morose and refused to go any farther or to disclose any information that would lead Hardt to the mine. Under the circumstances there seemed to be nothing else to do but abandon the search. The Indian set out for Tempe and Hardt returned to Payson.

Valentino died of a hemorrhage in Tempe one year later. The piece of rich ore he carried in the pocket of his leather chaps until it wore a hole in the leather, was ground in a mortar and panned out by Phil Fogle of Tempe who recovered a pill bottle almost full of coarse gold.

Henry Hardt, his good wife Rose, their three sons and daughter Gene are all going up to the Four Peaks country some day and have another look for the "Black Maverick" mine, still hidden somewhere in the canyon recesses high above the Valley of the Sun.

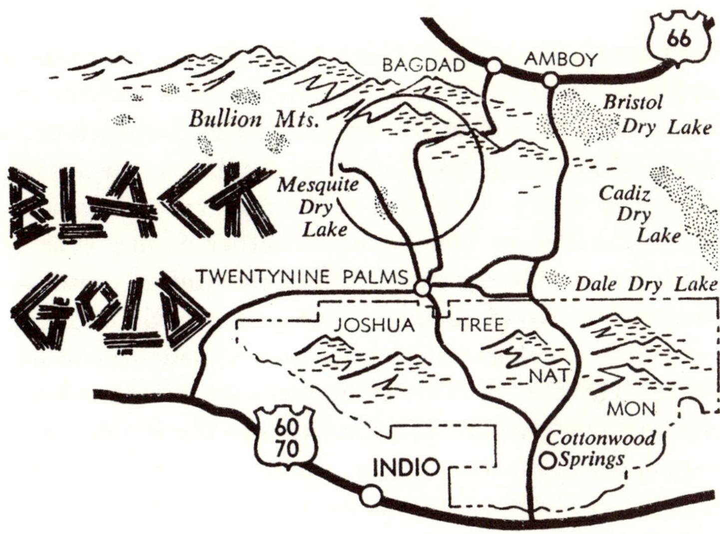

SOMEWHERE IN THE Bullion mountain country on the desert between Bagdad and Twentynine Palms, California, in the center of one of the many dry lakes known to exist there, stands a small black mountain in which there is said to be located, in the form of a chimney, another of the many lost mines of the Southwest.

The outcrop of this chimney has been broken down by erosion over a period of many thousands of years, scattering great quantities of gold nuggets over the barren ground around the foot of the mountain and among the rocks upon its sides. The nuggets, like the rocks and chunks of brown hematite of iron with which they are found, are all worn smooth. The old nuggets are covered over with a thin film of manganese oxide and can be distinguished from the hematite only by their darker color and greater specific gravity.

While many men, most of them Indians, are reported to

have seen this deposit, few of them have returned from the desert to tell the tale. Among the few said to have reached the mine and returned were two Indians and one white man. One of the Indians traded some of the black nuggets in Yuma. Pegleg Smith was in Yuma at the time and immediately started out to search for the mine. Whether Smith ever found the deposit is problematical. He lost the Indian's trail somewhere near Cottonwood springs, in San Bernardino county. Some time later Pegleg was found unconscious from hunger and thirst. He died in a coast hospital several days later without telling anyone where he found a large black gold nugget found in his possession. It is possible Smith may have found the nugget by the skeleton of another prospector who had reached the mine and died of heat and thirst on the way out.

For many years after the death of Pegleg Smith, strange stories continued to come out of the desert telling of dead Indians and large quantities of black gold scattered over the desert at the foot of a small black mountain in the center of a dry lake bed somewhere northwest of Cottonwood springs.

Many years later a white man arrived in San Gorgonio pass and stated he was going to seek the lost deposit of black gold.

Enlisting the aid of a partly civilized Indian who was less superstitious than other tribesmen, he cached food, water and grain for animals at intervals across the desert. After many months of preparation the two men set out across the desert in a buckboard pulled by two small Mexican mules. They camped each night at a station where food and water had been stored and after several days arrived at rimrock where the mesa dropped off abruptly almost a hundred feet and then sloped to the floor of a valley stretched out into the distance as far as the eye could see.

A narrow crevice was found in the steep wall and through this the mules were led down to the valley below. The buckboard was then dismantled and lowered over the cliff by the use of a windlass and long rope that had been brought along for the purpose. After loading the buckboard with food and water they again set out across this lower plain. After traveling two days their progress was halted by drifting sand dunes that blocked the progress of the mules and the wagon.

As the chimney-like mountain was now looming in the distance, it was decided to unhitch the mules and ride them the balance of the way. As they approached their destination they came upon a skeleton near which was an empty water gourd and a small pile of black gold nuggets.

Gathering the nuggets they continued to the foot of the black butte.

The igneous intrusion which formed the mountain was a jumbled mass of black heat-seared rocks interspersed here and there with large and small chunks of brown hematite of iron. Scattered around the foot of the mountain on the hard ground were thousands of small nuggets all worn smooth like the rocks and iron with which they were found. When the film of manganese was scraped off, beautiful yellow gold was disclosed.

Near the base of the mountain, thick beds of a yellowish powder were kept in a constant state of agitation by the winds that swirled over the little valley in which the pinnacle stood. The summit of the peak was cone-shaped and was full of kaolin and smooth pieces of hematite of iron. The hot rays of the sun beat down into the little valley and, reflected by the varnished rocks, made it almost like an oven. As the mysterious yellow dust settled on the prospectors' perspiring bodies it burned like fire, and when breathed into the lungs it almost choked them.

Since it would be impossible for them to remain for any length of time in such a place, the two men gathered as many of the gold nuggets as they could pack and after several hours arrived at the buckboard with gold they estimated to be worth $65,000. Before reaching the outer edge of the desert again their throats and lungs were parched from breathing the poisonous yellow powder and the skin of their hands and arms began to peel off. They finally reached civilization more dead than alive. It was many months before they recovered.

The proceeds of the trip were divided equally between the two partners. The white man purchased a small ranch in California. Neither of them ever made another trip to the valley of gold, but upon his deathbed a few years ago the white man told two old friends the secret of the black gold that is said to be guarded by the mysterious yellow powder and by the fierce heat of the desert itself.

FROM 1508 to 1648 the mine called the Virgin Guadalupe belonged to Tumacacori. It measured one league from the big door of the mission to the southwest, and from the waters of the San Ramon it measured 1800 varas to the north. Two hundred varas before arriving at the mine there is a black rock marked with a cross and the letters CCD-TD on the under side of the stone. Fifty varas from the cross of Christ to the south will be found slabs of virgin silver weighing from 25 to 250 pounds each. From here 200 varas in a southwesterly direction there are two peaks torn down by placing powder in the cliffs. The signs of the mine remain blotted out and people could pass over the rocks treading on the values and never see them.

The enclosure is 50 varas square covering up the treasure inside and outside of the mine. There are 2050 mule loads of virgin silver and 905 loads of gold and silver. The total value amounts to 45,000,000 pesos.

The above information was taken from an old document said to have been copied from church records in Spain. There is also a tradition among the Indians living in the vicinity of the mission that the mine was discovered by Indians in the year 1508, that it was being worked by them for its rich surface ores when the Spaniards landed their ships on the coast of Mexico in 1519, and that in 1540 Spaniards accompanying Coronado on his famous expedition to the north in quest of the golden treasures of the Seven Cities of Cibola found the Indians in possession of the fabulously rich mine. The Spaniards confiscated the mine and built a mission near the Indian temple. The mine was called the Virgin Guadalupe after their patron saint.

The Indians called their village Tumacacori (spelled Tumtacor on old Spanish maps in possession of the writer). The village and Indian temple were located about 25 miles northwest of the present ruins of the Tumacacori mission which was built in 1698 on the west bank of the Santa Cruz river because of the rich agricultural lands to be found there. The lower mission is located near the San Cayetano mountains and is often referred to by the Indians as Tumacacori de San Cayetano, in order to distinguish it from the upper mission which was located on the southern slopes of the Sierrita mountains and in a very rich mining district.

The lost Guadalupe has been sought persistently for many years in the vicinity of the lower mission by prospectors and adventurers who evidently were not aware of the fact that there were two Tumacacori missions. One man is said to have spent 12 years and $25,000 searching for the Guadalupe mine and the great treasure in the Tumacacori mountains to the west of the lower mission. This man is said to have had in his possession a copy of an old document copied from the church records in Spain, but like many others he did not know that there were two missions and that the Guadalupe and several other rich mines described in the old document are all located in the Sierrita mountains in the vicinity of the upper mission.

Extensive ruins on the southern slopes of the Sierritas and old caved workings in the vicinity indicate beyond a doubt that considerable mining operations were carried on there by the Indians and later by the Spaniards. Just why the mine was closed and abandoned in 1648 is unknown, but it is presumed to have been raided by the Indians in one of the numerous uprisings that occurred about then.

A considerable amount of treasure has, at different times, been found in and around the lower mission. This treasure consists of candlesticks, silver crosses and considerable bullion which was supposed to have been left by the Franciscan fathers when they abandoned the mission in 1823 because of the Mexican revolution and the accompanying Indian raids. However, the great treasure that has been so persistently sought by Mexicans and Americans alike for more than 80 years, is undoubtedly located in the vicinity of the upper and earlier mission, which according to tradition was built and destroyed sometime between the years 1540 and 1648. The mine is said to have been abandoned and the mountain peaks shot down over the mouth of the tunnel to conceal the rich ore and the vast treasure that had accumulated during the long years that the mine was worked by the Indians and later by the Spanish invaders.

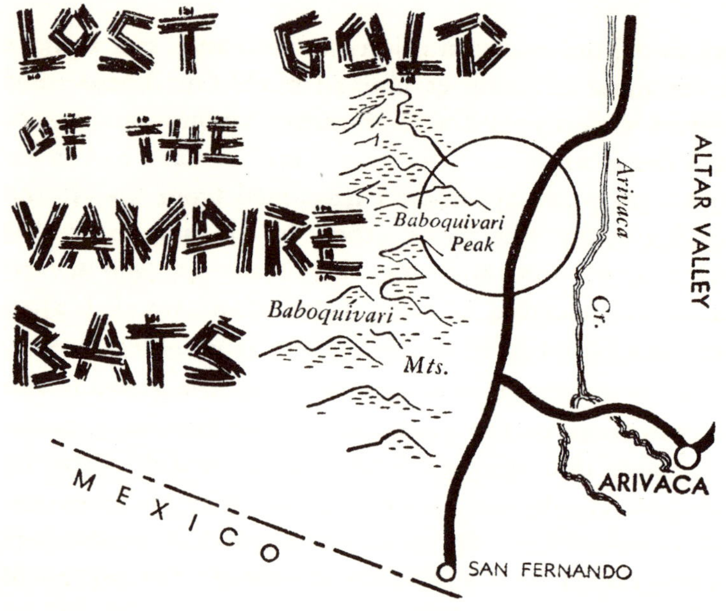

MORE THAN 75 YEARS have passed since the day an old Papago Indian tied his pinto to the hitch rack in front of the trading post in the little Mexican town of Arivaca, Arizona, and entered to barter gold nuggets for groceries and brightly colored calico.

Gambucinos were cleaning up an ounce or more of gold per day on Arivaca creek at that time, and the appearance of an Indian with a handful of large nuggets did not excite much curiosity.

However, as the years passed and the old Papago continued to make regular trips to the store, and as the placer along Arivaca creek grew leaner and leaner, the *gambucinos* began to take notice of the Indian and wonder where he got his gold. He had no visible means of support, was never seen to work a mine of any kind and always took life easy. He and his family never missed a fiesta at the old pueblo of Tucson and always seemed well supplied with money. As the years passed, the mystery deepened.

Luis Alvarado, an old Yaqui Indian who grew up in and around the Arivaca and Baboquivari country, remembered rumors of a rich gold mine that had been worked by the Spaniards in the Baboquivari foothills. The ruins of their houses still stand in the valley east of the Baboquivari mountains. Long rows of graves near the ancient foundations indicate the area once supported a large population.

Many believed that the Indian had found a rich placer or a cache of gold nuggets somewhere in the Baboquivari mountains near his brush hut. No amount of coaxing on the part of the merchant or the *gambucinos* around Arivaca could induce the old Papago to reveal the source of his wealth. Those who followed him always found their search ending at the hut —with no gold in sight. The mystery became more baffling when the old man moved his family to a new location on west Arivaca creek and still continued to barter gold with the trader in town.

The merchants had given up all hope ever of discovering his wealthy customer's secret. Then one day the Indian came in for his usual supply of groceries and, after paying the bill in gold, told the merchant that he had come to tell him the secret of the gold nuggets. "I am an old man," he said, "and I will not be able to make use of them much longer.

"Many years ago," he began, "while trailing a wounded deer across the foothills on the eastern slopes of the Baboquivari mountains, I sat down to rest on the top of a long ridge running in a northeasterly direction from the peak. As I rested, my attention was attracted by a flight of large vampire bats. They were emerging from a crevice not far from where I was sitting. Never in my life had I seen so many beautiful silver-colored bats of such size.

"I made a torch from a piece of dry ocotillo bark and threw it down into the crevice. From its dim light I could see what appeared to be a mine stope. Ore had been taken from so near the surface that the roof had broken through, creating an opening through which the bats might enter and leave the mine. A slight draft was coming from the opening, indicating that there was another entrance somewhere. I investigated further and discovered a small hole several hundred feet farther down the mountain side. Evidently it had been used by some wild animals for a den. It proved to be the portal of an old tunnel that had been covered over with mesquite poles and earth, now almost rotted away.

"After cleaning out the hole I made another torch and entered the tunnel," the Indian continued. "About 100 feet in, I came upon a number of metates and manos stacked against the wall. A short distance farther on was a pile of broken ore and some old mining tools and candlesticks such as were used by early Spanish miners. On the floor of one of the several large stopes was another pile of broken ore, and farther back against the wall stood a cross and a shrine such as Spaniards and Mexicans often build in mines they work. In a small tunnel or crosscut on one side of the long tunnel was a pile of buckskin bags full of gold nuggets. Evidently this gold had been recovered from some placer operations in another part of the mountain. Against the back end of the little tunnel a pile of gold bars gleamed yellow in the dim light of the torch. Some of the buckskin bags had rotted, and the nuggets had

The Indian waited until all the bats were back in the hole. Then he closed the entrance with rocks and earth.

trickled down, forming golden mounds on the floor of the tunnel.

"As I made my way out of the tunnel I stopped and picked up one of the buckskin bags of placer gold. I did not think the gods would object to an old Indian like myself taking one small bag of all that gold to buy food for himself and family. After concealing the tunnel entrance. I made my way down the mountainside to my house and buried the sack of gold beneath the dirt floor.

"It was from that sack," he explained to the trader, "that I got the gold I bartered with you for food and supplies. Go to the mountain, climb up the long ridge, and when late in the evening you see a large number of silver-colored bats in the air, you will be near the mine."

The merchant, mounted on his mule with his *mozo* running at his stirrup, left early the next day. Arriving late on the ridge he and the boy saw bats circling overhead and decided to wait until the next morning to search for the mine.

Just as daylight was breaking, the old Indian rode into camp. He seemed worried. He told the merchant he was frightened and regretted telling him the secret of the mine. A tribal law forbade any member of the tribe to disclose the location of a mine or treasure to an outsider. The Papago feared retribution at the hands of the gods.

"I waited until all the bats were back in the hole; then I closed the entrance with rocks and earth. No more bats," said the Indian. "They all will die in the hole, and no white man will ever find the mine."

No more vampire bats have ever been seen in the Baboquivari mountains. Nor has anyone ever found the lost mine they guarded.

Lost Adams Diggings

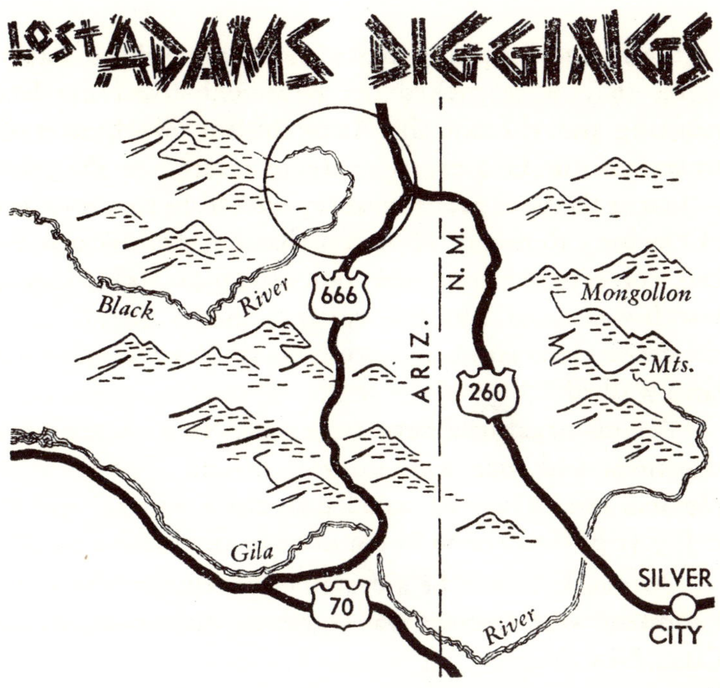

IN LIEUTENANT W. H. EMORY'S *Notes of a Military Reconnaissance from Fort Leavenworth in Kansas to San Diego in California*, published in 1848, is recorded: "The Prieto (Black) river flows down from the mountains freighted with gold. Its sands are said to be full of the precious metal. A few adventurers who ascended the river hunting beaver washed the sands at night when they halted and were richly rewarded. Tempted by their success, they made a second trip and were attacked and most of them killed by the Indians. My authority for this statement is Landreau, who, though an illiterate man, is truthful."

Landreau and a companion named Adams were survivors

of the ill-fated mining party. Heading south after the massacre, they were picked up in an exhausted condition by a scouting party from the Army of the West, near the headwaters of the Gila river. After the lapse of 20 years Adams returned to the Apache country and tried to relocate the ruins of the log cabin and the corral that he and his former partners had constructed near the rich diggings. The object of the search was about $60,000 worth of gold dust left buried under the cabin floor and the narrow gulch from which the gold had been washed.

Adams organized several expeditions to search for his old workings and was well known around Fort Wingate, New Mexico, where he purchased provisions and equipment for his many trips into the wild country to the southwest of the fort.

As nearly as can be ascertained the place where Adams and Landreau were rescued was about 25 miles northwest of Silver City, New Mexico. It was to this place that Adams came in later years, and he was often seen in that region.

The fact that the two men had traveled south after the massacre would indicate that the rich deposits were located near the headwaters of the Black river, but Adams had only a hazy recollection of the days when he and his companion wandered, exhausted and fearful of the Indians, from the scene of the attack.

Adams died at the age of 93 without relocating the gold. The search has continued to this day, and more than one man has lost his life on the trail in quest of the lost diggings.

If the story is true, the buckskin pokes, heavy with $60,000 in gold, still rot beneath the ashes of the old cabin floor. No doubt the place is now overgrown with vegetation, and only by mere accident will the treasure be recovered.

THE LOST ARCH placer diggings, said to be located about 40 miles south of Goffs and 25 miles north of Rice, in or near the north end of the Turtle mountains in eastern San Bernardino county, California, is another of the many mystery mines of the southwest. The now famous placer was first discovered by a small party of Mexican placer miners on their way across the mountains to the Colorado river placer diggings in the vicinity of La Paz. They camped one night on the wash to the east of the Old Woman mountains and somewhere near the north end of the Turtle range. There had been heavy rain; bunch grass grew along the edges of the wash, and small pools of clear water stood on the shallow bed rock.

The following morning while out looking for the hobbled pack mules the attention of the miners was attracted to the large amount of hematite of iron scattered over the mesa and along the wash. The soil on the ridges was red in color and from all appearances was good placer ground. A few pans of the dirt proved it to be rich in placer gold. Some of the samples yielded as much as five dollars' worth of gold to the pan.

Members of the party carried placer machines for the purpose of establishing themselves at the mines at La Paz, so it was decided to stay and work the new find. Accordingly, some of the men were sent down to La Paz for provisions while the others found a large pool of water that had collected from the recent rains and made adobes sufficient to construct a two-room house. As was their custom the Mexicans built the two rooms separately and extended the roof over the open space between them. The entrance to this open space was through a large adobe arch which Mexicans call a San Juan.

The new-found diggings proved to be very rich, and the Mexicans sluiced out $30,000 worth of gold before the hot weather dried up the waterholes. There was a small spring a few miles away, later known as Coffin springs, but it did not furnish enough water to carry on sluicing operations. In view of the scarcity of water it was decided to store the equipment and return the following season and continue their operations.

Reaching Los Angeles, the party split up, some going north to the Mother Lode country and others returning to Mexico. No maps had been drawn of the placer field, and later when separate members of the party sought to relocate the placer field they were unsuccessful.

In time the contents of the adobe house were carried away by Mojave Indians and the house itself fell down, all except the arch doorway. The arch was still standing as late as 1900 and was seen by the late Peter Kohler, who did not know of the existence of the rich placer diggings.

According to another version of the story, the placer was named after a natural arch of earth or rock standing over the upper end of a deep gulch running down from the east side of the Turtle mountains. This is very unlikely as the terrain does not lend itself to the formation of that kind of a natural arch.

The adobe arch has now been leveled by erosion, and the location can only be identified by some of the broken and rusted contents of the old adobe house that are still scattered over the desert near where it once stood. An old tub found there in later years caused the diggings to be known as the Lost Tub placer.

It was later discovered that the hematite scattered over the desert below the old house carried about $100 a ton in gold, showing free gold when broken open. The red ironstained gravel on the ridges and along the wash is still rich in placer gold and would return a handsome profit.

Many expeditions have set out from Los Angeles and Yuma to search for the lost diggings. No doubt many of the searchers have seen this red mesa thickly strewn with boulders of hematite of iron but have never associated them with the Lost Arch placer diggings.

LOST PIMA INDIAN GOLD

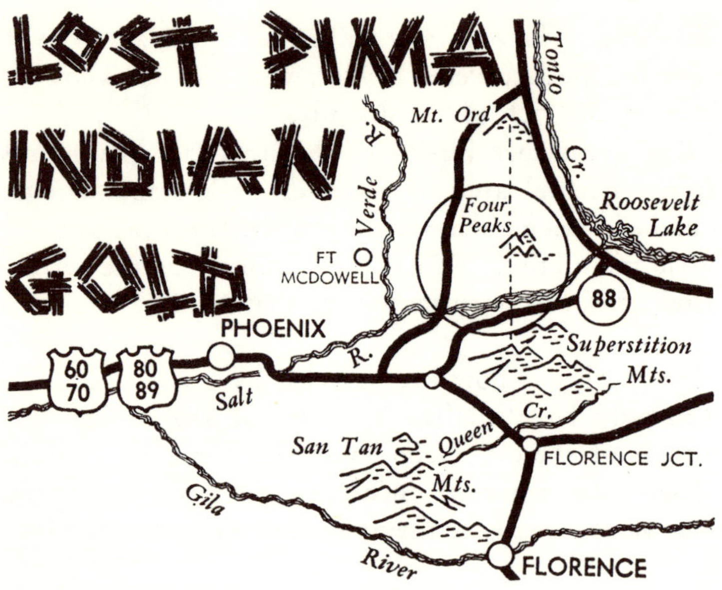

MANY YEARS AGO, a party of eastern bear hunters engaged a group of young Pima Indians to guide them into the Mount Ord country 50 miles northeast of Phoenix, Arizona.

The easterners planned to spend several weeks hunting in the area, and when the Indian guides had seen them comfortably established in the wilderness camp, they started back to the reservation. To shorten the distance home, they traveled in a straight line from the southern base of Mount Ord to the northern foothills of the Superstition mountains. They had been well paid for the trip and, in a merry mood, they traveled fast, single file, chanting their tribal songs as they hurried along.

While passing through the high rocky ground a few miles

north of the Superstition mountains, the young bucks suddenly came upon two skeletons. Upon closer examination, they appeared to be white men, probably prospectors. The bones had bleached white from long exposure to the elements and lay over a considerable area, evidently disturbed by coyotes and carrion birds. Nearby lay a number of old brass shells of the large caliber used in guns of that early period in the West. A few badly rusted cooking utensils, mining tools and other pieces of camp equipment lay scattered over the ground near a shallow mining shaft. On one side of the rude working was a pile of ore containing yellow metal that sparkled in the sunlight. Thinking the rock might be of some use to tribal craftsmen, the bucks gathered a few of the large pieces to take home with them.

It was late afternoon when they again set out for the reservation. They skirted the sandy lands on the west side of the Superstitions and by late evening arrived at an ancient waterhole between Queen creek and the north end of the San Tan mountains. They stopped here to quench their thirst and to rest for the night.

Just before sunset, an old prospector came to the waterhole to fill his kegs and water his burros. The animals drank their fill and stood dozing in the warm light from the setting sun, while the prospector busied himself filling the kegs and making ready to return to his camp high in the foothills of the Superstitions.

His tasks done, he stopped to chat with the young Pimas who were preparing their evening meal of small game they had killed along the way. Seeing the pile of ore that the Indians had carelessly thrown on the ground, the old man casually picked up a few pieces and was surprised to find them flecked with bright yellow gold. Not wishing to excite the Pimas and hoping to disguise from them the value of their find, he threw the ore on the ground. "It's no good," he told the bucks, and advised them to throw it away.

The next morning when the prospector returned to the waterhole the Indians were gone; but he was delighted to find they had left a few pieces of the ore behind. After watering his burros again, he gathered up the rich samples and hurried back to his camp in the mountains. He ate a hasty meal, then saddled one of his burros and set out to backtrack the Indians to where they had found the ore, the shallow shaft and the two skeletons they had told him about the night before.

He found the trail easy to follow until he came to the high rocky country north of the Superstitions, where it disappeared among barren boulders. He rode in circles, cutting for signs, but was unable to find any tracks beyond the desert's edge and the soft sand. It was growing late, and the tired old man reluctantly decided to return to camp for the night and later plan another trip into the high rock ground that lay beyond the desert to the north.

Anxious to know what the ore would run in gold, he took the samples to the assay office in Phoenix. Joe Porterea, an old-time assayer well known to many pioneers of the state, tested the gold-studded quartz, and the certificate he turned over to the prospector showed that it ran $35,000 per ton in gold and showed every evidence of having come from the country where the Pimas said they had found it—between Mount Ord and the northern slopes of the Superstitions.

After celebrating his good fortune for several days, the old man returned to his camp to plan a campaign that would enable him to keep the secret of the mine while locating the old shaft and reap its benefits for himself.

In the years that followed, he managed to guard his secret and to live off the country while he searched the rocky wilds for the lost gold. Finally, when too old and feeble to face the continued hardships of life alone in the desert, he revealed the secret to others. Several took up the search, but like the old prospector, they never were able to locate the right place.

Disillusioned and broke, the old man spent the last years of his life hanging around saloons and gambling houses in Phoenix, where he earned many a free drink or a good meal by showing the small pieces of rich quartz and telling his story to new arrivals in the frontier town.

Evidently the old man had not lived in the West long enough to learn that Indians, traveling on foot or on horseback, often follow a straight course. By drawing a straight line on a map from the north end of the Superstitions to the southern slopes of Mount Ord and then prospecting along both sides of the line, he might have located the lost ledge.

Another story seems to explain the construction of the crude mine shaft and the two whitened skeletons the young Pima guides found near it.

One day, during the time United States soldiers were stationed at Fort McDowell in the Apache country north of Phoenix, two soldiers went out deer hunting across the Verde river east of the fort. They returned that evening loaded down with all the rich gold ore they could carry. The ore was a white milky quartz generously flecked with free gold; the metal recovered from it was sold in Phoenix for $1400. Soon after the two soldiers returned to the high rocky location between the Superstitions and Mount Ord, but they were unable to find the white ledge they had discovered while trailing a wounded deer that day and from which they had broken the rich ore.

After being discharged from the army, the soldiers are believed to have made their way back into the country and again taken up the search for the lost ledge. The skeletons found by the young Indian guides most likely were theirs. Successful in rediscovering the gold lode, they probably had been killed by Apache renegades hiding out in the caves of the Superstitions long after Geronimo and his band of warriors had been rounded up and placed on reservations.

There are yet a few old Pimas on the Sacaton reservation along the Gila river who were members of the guide party which first found the soldiers' ore. They might have led the old prospector back to the rich gold lode, but he selfishly kept his secret until he no longer could hope to benefit from it.

LOST SILVER OF THE JESUITS

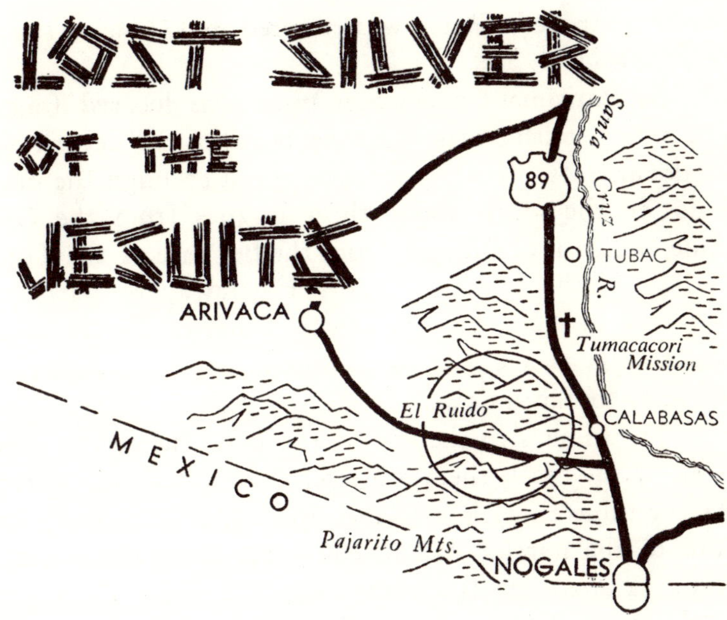

OLD CHURCH RECORDS brought from Spain by Don Ricardo Ortiz of Hermosillo, Sonora, Mexico, and Don Santiago Diaz, former governor of Lower California, state that La Purisima Concepcion was one of the richest mines ever discovered by the Indians of Pimeria Alta, as this part of the country was called by the early Spaniards.

Pieces of rich native silver float and the outcrop of the vein were discovered by the Opata Indians in 1508, about 15 years before the Spaniards beached their ships on the east coast of Mexico. The mine was taken over by the Spaniards upon their arrival in what is now Arizona and New Mexico, and was being operated by them in 1750 when the second revolt of the Pima tribes occurred. The missions were plundered and partly destroyed. Peace was restored in 1752 and the missions reoccupied in 1754.

"La Purisima Concepcion mine was located four leagues (12 miles) south of the Tumacacori mission," record old Spanish documents. "Follow straight ahead through the pass of Los Janos to the south about three leagues from the Guadalupe mine, which is one league from the big gate of the Tumacacori mission to the south, to another gateway or pass called the Gateway to Agua Hondo (Deep Water). To the south from this pass runs a creek that empties onto the desert near the old town of Santa Cruz.

"The mine is to the east of the pass. Below the pass on the bank of the creek there are twelve arrastres and twelve patios. At the mine there is a tunnel 300 varas (835 feet) long that runs to the north. About 200 varas from the portal of this tunnel a cross-cut 100 varas long leads from the main tunnel to the west. The ore in the face of this crosscut is yellow and is one-half silver and one-fifth gold.

"Fifty varas from the mouth of the mine in a southerly direction will be found *planchas de plata* (slabs or balls of silver) weighing from 25 to 250 pounds each. In the rock above the tunnel is the name La Purisima Concepcion, cut with a chisel. The mouth of the tunnel is covered by a copper door and fastened with a large iron lock."

There is a mass of evidence to indicate that this old mine is located in the narrow pass between the west end of the Pajarito mountains and El Ruido (mountain of the noises). Years ago a saloon keeper in Nogales grubstaked an old prospector to search for gold and silver in and around the Pajarito and El Ruido mountains. The old fellow was gone about six weeks and then one day he appeared in front of the saloon with

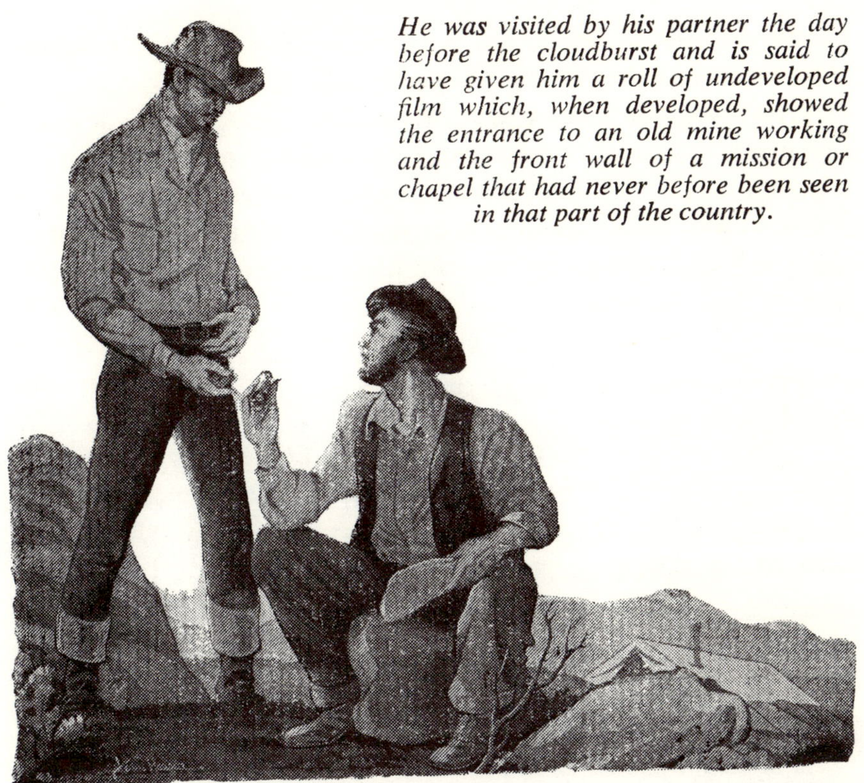

He was visited by his partner the day before the cloudburst and is said to have given him a roll of undeveloped film which, when developed, showed the entrance to an old mine working and the front wall of a mission or chapel that had never before been seen in that part of the country.

two burros loaded down with large chunks of native silver he had found scattered over the surface of the ground in the pass between the Pajaritos and El Ruido. They are believed to have eroded from some kaolin outcrops that are known to exist in the pass. The old man started to celebrate his good fortune and was found dead the next morning. The saloon keeper was never able to find the place where the old prospector picked up the rich pieces of silver.

Shortly after the conclusion of the Mexican war and the signing of the Gadsden treaty when the tri-color was moved southward, an old prospector with headquarters at Tubac made frequent trips to the Pajaritos and El Ruido and each time returned with large pieces of native silver. It is said upon good authority that only a few years ago a prospector camped in the pass and after prospecting a week or two his camp was washed away by a cloudburst that sent a wall of water down the creek near where he had pitched his tent. Presumably he was washed away with it, as no trace of him ever has been found.

He was visited by his partner the day before the cloudburst and is said to have given him a roll of film, which when developed showed the entrance to an old mine working and the front wall of an old mission or chapel that had never before been seen in this part of the country. The little church was probably a *visita* for Tumacacori mission and was not unlike those frequently built by Spanish-American miners in the vicinity of the mines in which they are employed. From the evidence it would seem that La Purisima Concepcion mine really existed and that it was very rich.

Tumacacori was founded in 1691, but just how long the Jesuit fathers worked the mines is unknown. They were, however, working a number of gold and silver mines in the mountains around the mission in 1767, when King Charles III issued the edict expelling the Jesuits from Spain and all its possessions.

Foreseeing that they would be unable to take any of their treasure with them, the Jesuits are said to have buried it near the missions or in the mines, hoping that they would be able to return for it at a future date. They never returned to claim their property, and many of the mines and treasures remain undiscovered to this day.

That the Jesuits of Tumacacori, while spreading the doctrine of Christ, carried on extensive mining operations and collected much gold and silver is indicated by the recent discovery of a number of adobe smelters *(vasos)* on the east side of the mission. Two thousand fifty mule loads of virgin silver and 205 loads of gold bullion are said to have been taken from Tumacacori mission by the padres and concealed in the Guadalupe mine which measured one league southwest of the mission ruins.

In view of the fact that so much native silver float has been found in the pass and at the Planchas de Plata mine a short distance to the south in Sonora, Mexico, it is the belief of the writer that the story of the Pure Conception mine as set forth in the old document is a true one. Mexican and Indian vaqueros believe El Ruido is haunted and avoid it as much as possible. I once rode a mule across the foothills of El Ruido and owing to the peculiar nature of the rock his hoof-beats sounded like a bass drum.

The kaolin outcroppings in the pass between the Pajaritos and El Ruido would seem to offer a clue to the origin of the rich pieces of native silver that have from time to time been discovered on the surface. The padres in their old records often mention having found native silver in veins of kaolin or *caliche*, as they called it.

These outcrops consist of kaolin, iron-stained quartz and occasionally large nuggets of native silver. Most of the rich minerals originally contained in these veins have been leached and carried down to water-level and precipitated as secondary enrichment. It is not uncommon in the desert country to find rich outcrops of silver ore near the surface while directly under them the ore has been leached out. Many of the old Spanish workings were stopped in this leached zone instead of going on down to water-level for the secondary enrichment that is almost certain to be found under these leached zones.

Many of these old workings that were closed down when they entered the leached zone, or were later closed and abandoned upon the demonitization of silver, could be re-opened today and made to produce millions in silver and copper ore. Most of the silver mines in southern Arizona carry a high percentage of copper.

LOST DUTCHMAN MINE

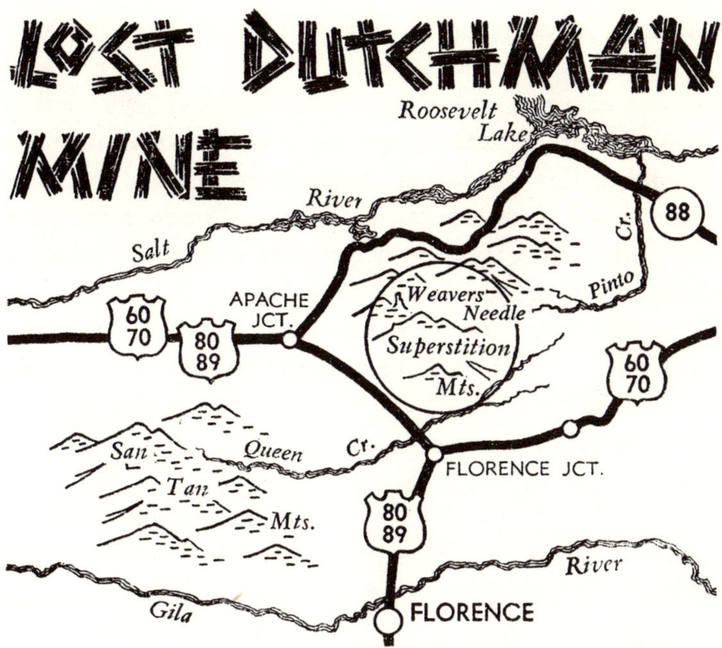

JACOB WALZ has become one of the legendary figures of the Southwest. Unlike the mountain men who trapped the streams and traded with the Indians during the middle of the 19th century, Walz was a miner.

If we are to believe the tales told about him following his arrival in Phoenix about 1864, his life was a series of episodes of high adventure. He is best known, however, for his asserted connection with the Peralta gold mine, said to be located somewhere in the recesses of the barren and fantastic Superstition mountains 25 miles east of Phoenix.

Don Miguel Peralta is said to have discovered the rich vein some time in the early '50s while prospecting the rugged Superstitions. Peralta was later joined by his friend Don Francisco Ballesteros of Sonora, Mexico.

Beautiful ornaments fashioned from solid gold found in recent years in the graves of a prehistoric Indian village in Garden valley in the Superstitions, would indicate that the rich ledge was known and worked by an ancient tribe which lived in that part of the country long before the arrival of the Spanish invaders.

Recruiting a crew of miners and packers among the Mexicans and Indians, Peralta and Ballesteros built an arrastre and opened the vein.

The ore was exceedingly rich. It was put in leather bags and packed on the backs of mules to the arrastre where it was ground. As the gold was freed from the quartz it was collected in the form of amalgam which was smelted into bars in a small adobe furnace.

An adobe house with a rock foundation was built along one side of the boulder strewn canyon about one mile below the mine. Near the house and camp a rock corral was built for the mules.

With an abundance of rich ore, and the bars of gold piling higher day by day, there is no reason to believe that the two old friends were unhappy. With the lofty Superstitions towering high above them in the deep blue Arizona sky, it can hardly be denied that they had found a beautiful place in which to live and work. Only one thing threatened their security—the fierce Apaches, whose hand was against everyone.

The ore grew richer and richer as the inclined shaft penetrated deeper and deeper into the mountain side. To avoid the necessity of hoisting the ore up the shaft it was decided to run a tunnel into the mountain from near the canyon. Accordingly the tunnel was started and had reached a distance of about 50 feet when the mine was suddenly attacked by a large number of Apache warriors. Surprised and greatly outnumbered, the little band of miners and packers was almost completely wiped out.

Only one man escaped. This Mexican hid in the rocky canyon and then made his way to the arrastre where Peralta, Ballesteros and the two Peralta boys were grinding ore. Taking their rifles and ammunition the five men hurried into the hills from where finally, after enduring many hardships, they made their way back to Sonora.

Some of the ore-laden pack mules were stampeded during the massacre and disappeared in the hills. Years later, two old prospectors, known as "Silverlocks" and "Goldenlocks," found some of the rich ore in a box canyon where it evidently had fallen from the packs of the straying animals. Knowing nothing of the Peralta mine tragedy, the prospectors assumed the ore came from a ledge in the vicinity where it was found, and dug many holes and trenches in an effort to locate the vein.

Jacob Walz, traveling in Mexico, is said to have heard the story from the survivors of the massacre and to have made his way north to the little frontier town of Florence on the Gila river, arriving there in the early '70s. He outfitted himself and headed his little pack train into the wild Superstitions to search for the Peralta workings, which were said to have been covered up by the Apache Indians after the massacre to prevent them from again falling into the hands of the white man.

A month later Jacob Walz reappeared in Florence looking for someone to make a dry washer or rocker small enough to be packed on the back of a burro. He was directed to another German known only as Frank, who was making his living doing odd jobs of carpenter work around Florence. While the placer machine was being completed Walz told the carpenter he had found some very rich placer gravel near Iron mountain on a branch of Pinto creek and that he was prospecting upstream to find the vein from which the gold came.

On his next trip to Florence Walz told Frank he had found the old Peralta workings from which the placer gold had eroded. Walz invited Frank to go with him and help work the mine. Knowing nothing about mining and being afraid of the Apaches, the young carpenter refused to go.

Later Jacob Walz was joined by a nephew named Jacob Weizer. The two men made frequent trips into the Superstitions, always returning with their burros loaded down with rich gold ore which was sold in Phoenix, Tucson and Florence.

Old Frank, who later lived in the Pioneers' Home in Prescott, said the location of the much hunted mine did not seem to be much of a secret in those days and that many old timers like himself knew that it was located somewhere on Pinto creek not far from Iron mountain.

Walz was not a naturalized citizen of the United States and for that and other reasons did not have his find recorded. One of the Poston brothers and a man named Myers of Tucson bought some of the ore from Walz and tried to follow him to the mine, losing the trail at Whitlow's ranch on upper Queen creek on the south side of the Superstitions.

One day when returning to the mine Walz and Weizer saw two men breaking ore on the dump. The men were very dark and were taken to be Apaches. Shooting from behind some large boulders the Germans killed both men. Closer examination revealed that the two men were Mexicans, who evidently had come from Mexico to relocate the mine. The bodies of the dead men were taken to a nearby wash and covered with earth and rocks.

Later Weizer was caught in a flood while attempting to cross the Gila river and after being rescued by Pima Indians died from exposure. The body was buried somewhere on the old J. D. Walker ranch on the Gila river.

Walz, now an old man and left alone, made his last trip to the mine in 1877. After filling his sacks with the fabulously rich ore the old Dutchman covered the entrance to the shaft with timbers and rocks, loaded the sacks on his burros and then headed down the canyon never to return.

Walz sorted out a few rich specimens to keep as souvenirs and sold the balance of the ore in Phoenix. With the proceeds of the sale the old man built a small adobe house in the flat country near the Salt river where he lived for a number of years.

In February 1891 a great flood came down the Salt river and washed the little house away. Walz was rescued but soon died from an illness brought on by exposure. He was then 84 years of age and took the secret of the exact location of the mine with him to his grave.

There are many versions of the Lost Dutchman mine and as usual many "true" maps have made their appearance since Walz passed away. Some of these maps place the location of the mine in the vicinity of Weavers Needle, where since Walz' death most of the searching has been carried on. In addition to the 4 men killed in the massacre, many others have lost their lives in the Superstition mountains. Often these searchers were inexperienced and died from hunger and thirst. Others no doubt were murdered for the information they were supposed to have.

Unlike the ancient Indian tribes who built their villages in the little valleys, the modern red man has almost fanatical fear of the Superstitions and refuses to go near them. It is undoubtedly true that recesses in the forbidden Superstitions contain the yellowing bones and grinning skulls of many Indians and white men who have lost their lives there. However, it would seem to the writer that if the searchers for the Lost Dutchman mine would disregard some of the old superstitions and confine their operations to the mineralized country around Iron mountain in the vicinity of Pinto creek, they might be rewarded with success and again bring to light the millions in rich ore said to be stored away in the Lost Dutchman mine.

LOST CAPT. DICK MINE

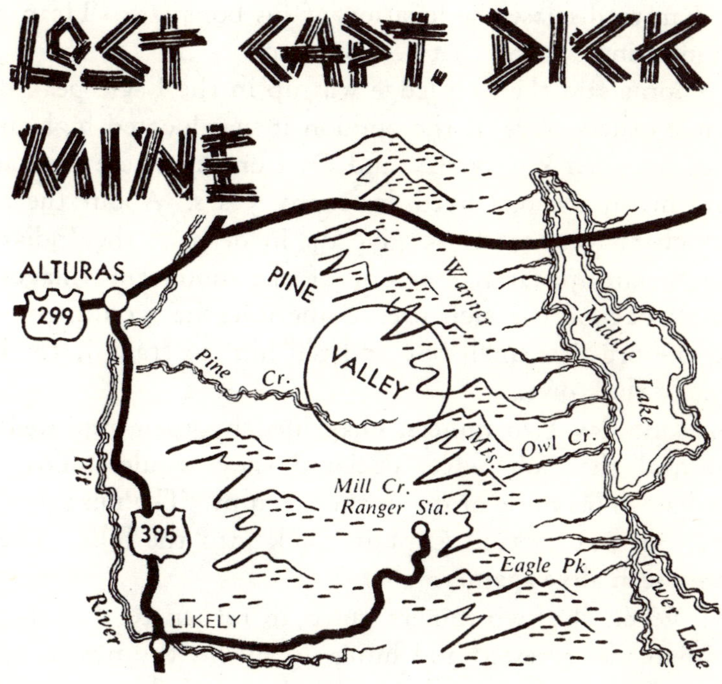

FOR ALMOST A hundred years the story of an outcrop of rich gold ore has circulated through the mining country in northeastern California, its fabulous richness sometimes believed, more often ridiculed.

Not until an old Indian locally known as Captain Dick came down from his home on Owl creek and started bartering large chunks of extremely rich gold ore for loaves of bread, was the story lifted out of the legendary class.

One look at the ore was enough to stampede the most experienced prospector or desert rat into the hills to search for the ledge. But no amount of coaxing would induce the old

Indian to disclose the location of his bonanza. "Heap far over mountains" was all that he would say.

Some said the rich ledge was up in the Eagle peak country, while others were of the opinion it was located high up in the pass between Pine valley and Owl creek, where Captain Dick and his squaw had lived for many years. About the time the searchers were ready to give up in despair, the Indian would put in an appearance at one of the mountain villages with a small bag of the rich ore. Sometimes he would give a piece of the ore to a small boy and tell him to trade it for bread at one of the stores.

One day two miners, chagrined by their repeated failures to find the rich ledge, declared they would follow the old Indian to his mine or die in the attempt. The next day the two men set out to trail Captain Dick into the hills. They never were seen alive again.

When the two miners failed to return to their homes, the Indian was arrested and hung up by his thumbs in an unsuccessful effort to make him talk. Later vigilantes took him out of jail and hanged him.

Shortly after his death, a German prospector offered to marry the Indian's widow in an effort to learn where the ore came from. She refused to marry the desert rat and would give no information other than to say that she knew the location and that Captain Dick had told her to keep the secret.

After the woman died, a drunken sheepherder in a talkative mood told a friend that once, while driving his flock of sheep down through the high pass between Pine valley and Owl creek, he saw the old Indian emerge from a small hole on the mountainside with a small bag in one hand. After looking around to make sure no one was watching him, the Indian

The next day the two men set out to trail Captain Dick into the hills and were never seen alive again.

moved a large flat rock over the small opening and then disappeared down the mountainside.

The herder said he took a candle with him the next day and

while his sheep were grazing nearby, he crawled into the hole from which he had seen the old Indian emerge. The small opening widened into a tunnel the ceiling of which was threaded with gold seams. Breaking off a few pieces of the heavy rock he put them in his lunch sack and by the dim light of his candle made his way along the tunnel.

Suddenly the flickering light disclosed two grinning skulls hanging from pegs that had been driven into crevices in the ore in the face of the tunnel. In the space between the two skulls the grey-colored rock was matted together with large chunks and wires of gleaming gold. Never in his life had he seen anything like it. Frightened by the gruesome discovery he made his way out of the death chamber and replaced the flat rock over the entrance. The few small pieces of ore he carried away were sold for $1400.

The herder, knowing that the squaw was dead, quit his job and disappeared into the mountains. Several weeks went by and then one day he appeared on the streets dressed up and apparently well supplied with money. When he had squandered the money he slipped away in the night making his way to the tunnel for more gold. This went on for several months. When the herder in a drunken mood offered to show a new found friend the mine for a small loan with which to buy more liquor, the friend, not having heard of the magic tunnel, refused the loan.

The herder later disappeared from his usual haunts and never was seen again. There are those who say he was followed to the hills and that he met the same fate as the two miners whose skulls he found hanging in the face of the tunnel.

The friend who refused the loan has joined other desert rats in looking for the mine ever since. Year in and year out the search for one of California's most famous lost mines goes on. It would be hard to make these old-timers believe there is anything less than a million dollars worth of gold in the Captain Dick tunnel.

Some of the oldest inhabitants in the Warner range believe the Captain Dick mine is no other than the famous long lost Cement mine, said to have been found by three young German brothers who in 1841 survived an Indian massacre on the great plains, and after making their way westward into northwestern Nevada or northeastern California, found an outcropping of conglomerate of natural cement which was heavily impregnated with gold nuggets.

Each of the brothers took 25 pounds of the ore and started south toward the Spanish settlements along the coast. After enduring untold hardships, one of the brothers got out alive with his 25 pounds of ore and learned it was worth $200 a pound.

It is believed that some of the old Indians around Alturas and Likely know the location of the long lost tunnel, but like Captain Dick and his squaw, refuse to lead the searchers to it.

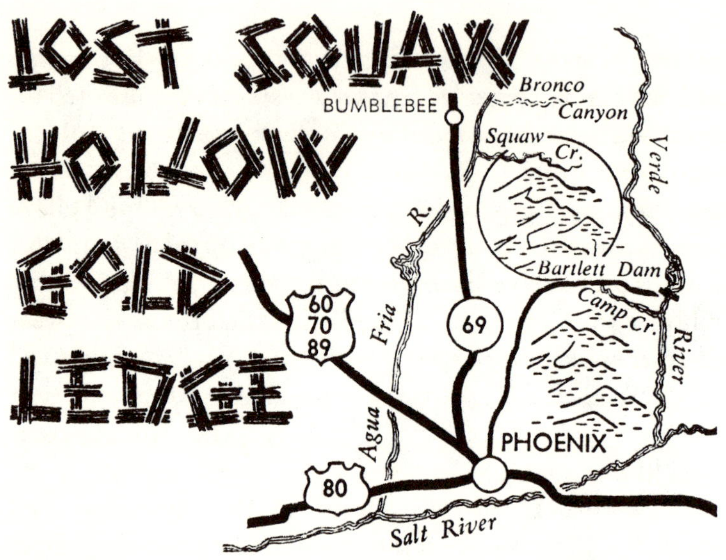

THE STORY OF THE LOST Squaw Hollow gold ledge is well authenticated. The ledge was discovered by a number of pioneer Arizona Indian fighters who broke ore from the rich ledge and carried it to their camp in Squaw Hollow, about 40 miles north of Phoenix, Arizona, in the Camp creek country and about 10 miles south of Bronco canyon.

In 1864 Judge J. T. Alsap, in company with a small number of pioneers under the command of Colonel Woolsey, whose Indian fighting proclivities are well known to all old-timers in Arizona, pitched their camp in Squaw Hollow after an engagement with a small band of Apache warriors. Following the fight, some of the men prospected for gold in the nearby hills. Their efforts were highly successful according to the story, and a few hours later the prospectors returned to camp with a hatful of the richest gold ore the judge had ever seen.

But Apache warriors returned with reinforcements, and Woolsey and his little band of fighters were so outnumbered they retreated without having left any markers as a guide to the gold discovery. Later those who knew about the gold strike became separated, and it was many years before the Apaches were completely subdued and the way opened for mining operations. The location of the gold had remained a secret because all of them had expected to return at a later date to make legal claim to the gold ledge.

Not having been with the prospectors, the judge did not know the exact location of the gold. But after the Apache warfare was ended he returned to the region to search for it. He made his headquarters at Camp creek and spent many days prospecting the area. He was sure none of his companions had returned to re-locate the rich quartz ledge, for he found no mines or prospect holes in the area.

Years later, an old Mexican sheepherder, driving his flocks down from the hills into Salt river valley camped one night in Squaw Hollow with a man who had built a cabin and was working a rich gold mine in the vicinity. The prospector was bringing his ore out on burros, grinding it in a large iron mortar and washing it in the creek. Reporting the incident later, the sheepherder said the man told him he was sending the gold east to put his son through college.

The sheepherder did not learn the name of the prospector and when he returned to Squaw Hollow in later years he did not find him there, nor did he see any mine workings in the vicinity. A small pile of tailings near the ruins of the cabin was all that remained. He did not search for the ledge, but remembered the rich ore he had seen at the cabin, and told the story to a friend who was interested in mining.

The whole country in the vicinity of Camp creek and Squaw Hollow is thickly overgrown with manzanita brush and unless an outcropping of quartz is large enough to stand out above the brush it would be very difficult to locate. Whether the ledge discovered by the Indian fighters and the one later worked by the lone prospector are the same would be hard to say.

Squaw Hollow is located in a highly mineralized country and is a good place to camp. Because of the character of the country, it is easily possible that the original gold strike has escaped the notice of passing prospectors through the intervening years, and remains hidden somewhere in the brush.

THE SILVER STAIRWAY

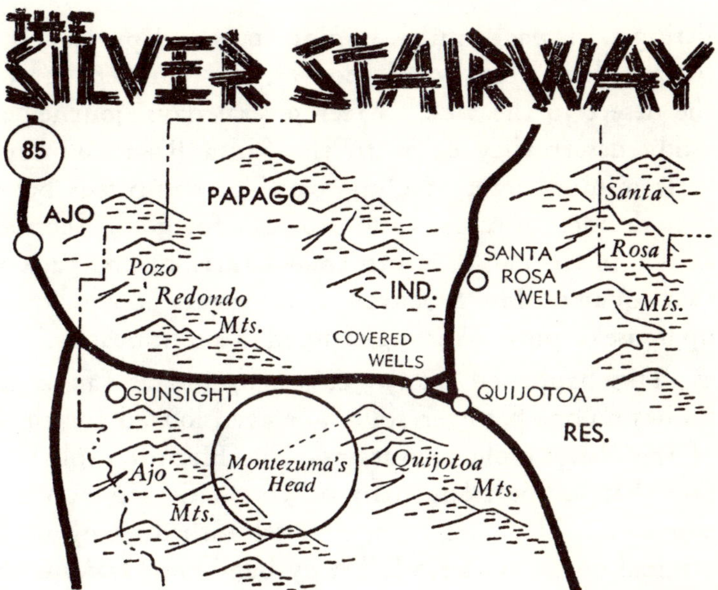

WOULD YOU LIKE TO OWN a beautiful palace with a silver stairway? Here is the story of a man who built one from ore he found on the Arizona desert. Enough for another palace or two still lies at his bonanza site, awaiting the desert rat or prospector lucky enough to find it.

It was shortly after the Civil war when a man whom we will call James Sterling set out across the great plains, then infested with hostile Indians, in search of health and wealth. He planned to prospect for gold and silver in the mountains of the west. After prospecting in many parts of the country, he came finally to Arizona.

Soon after arriving at the old Pueblo of Tucson, Sterling was joined by another man by the name of John Smith. Outfitting with pack mules, mining tools and provisions sufficient to last them for several months, the partners set out across the desert to the west. After several days' journey across the sandy desert they came to the Santa Rosa country and the little mining town of Quijotoa. The camp was booming and they decided to remain and prospect for gold. Soon after their arrival in the camp, Smith traded three of the pack mules for two squaws. He procured a one-room adobe house and set up housekeeping. Sterling camped in a tent nearby.

This happened many years ago, and as far as the writer knows no one has ever found, or even looked for the lost ledge of the Sheep Hole mountains. The Hermit probably met the fate that has befallen many others on the desert wastes of the Southwest, his bones lying covered with drifting sands. If the original operators were killed by bandits or Indians they probably left some treasure buried in or around their small rock house, the ruins of which probably still stand.

The two partners located some placer claims which proved to be exceedingly rich, and they profited greatly from their operations. Having grown wealthy, they decided to dissolve the partnership and strike out each for himself.

Sterling, now much improved in health, continue to prospect for gold and silver in the surrounding mountains. One day while on his way across the desert between Quijotoa and Gunsight, his attention was attracted to a large number of brown colored boulders scattered over the floor of a small valley or slight depression in the lava flow that covers that part of the country. The rocks proved to be unbelievably rich in native silver in the form of large plates and wires. There was no sign of a ledge to which the large pieces of ore could have belonged, and the fact that they were so large precluded the possibility of their having been left there by some old Spanish *conducta* that had been attacked by Apache Indians forcing them to unload the ore and leave it there.

The deposit was duly claimed by Sterling and the ore broken up and transported on the backs of mules to Yuma on the Colorado river, from where it was transported to the gulf, loaded on sailing vessels and shipped east. Sterling, now a wealthy man, followed the shipment back to his old home in the east, and with the proceeds of the ore and his placer operations at Quijotoa he built a beautiful mansion on the edge of a lake. The stairway leading from the first to the second and third floors was fashioned from massive plates of solid silver that had been smelted from the rich ore he had found on the far-away Arizona desert.

A line drawn from the north end of the Quijotoa mountains southwest to the top of Montezuma's Head will pass through the little valley or depression where Sterling found the great pile of float matted together with native silver. An arroyo enters through the east side of the little valley and has its outlet a short distance away in the southwest side of the depression.

From all indications, it appears to the writer that the ore came from pieces of float broken from a nearby ledge now completely covered over by the lava flow. Water entering the little arroyo during the rainy season cut out the soft porous lava rock and carried it out through the opening in the southwest side of the valley, exposing the pieces of rich float and leaving them stranded on the floor of the little depression. The large blocks of quartz were rough, indicating they had not traveled far from the parent ledge or deposit before they slid down the gentle slope.

LOST BLUE BUCKET GOLD

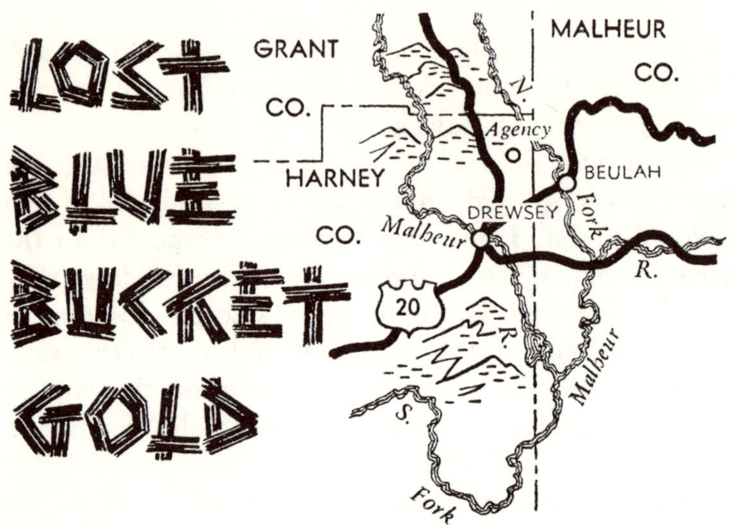

IN THE YEAR 1845, four years before the California gold rush, an emigrant train was on its way across the great plains. Oregon, not California was its goal, land, not gold, its guiding star.

The pioneers worked their way across the country with the aid of a compass. They crossed desert, plain and mountains keeping on a fairly straight course. If a large mountain stood in their way, they crossed instead of detouring around it. Finally they reached Gravelly Ford crossing on the Humboldt river, at the present site of Beowawe, Nevada. Here they split up into two parties. One party continued along the Humboldt river, while the other group struck due north by way of the Black Rock mountains. From the latter party a strange tale originated years later.

Leaving the Black Rock mountains behind, the wagon train came to a high mountain range. The approaching slopes were gradual, and the party managed to reach the top with all the wagons. From this high point the wagon boss got a good view of the surrounding country and took bearings on the Twin Sister peaks. The west side of the mountain was found to be very steep. In those days lock chains were used as brakes, and they would not serve here. Heavy timbers were cut and chained to the several wagons, and in that manner they made their way down.

While the wagons were being taken down the mountain-side, camp was made at a spring in the canyon below. Some of the members of the party, gathering wood for the camp-fire, picked up pieces of metal that looked to them like brass. These people were farmers and knew very little about gold. They did not recognize the "pretty yellow rocks" as rich gold nuggets. The children picked up quite a few of the "pebbles" to play with. Several buckets were filled with them. The buckets, like the wagons, were painted blue.

While camped at the little spring, one of the women in the party became sick and died. They buried her near the spring, heaping up rocks on the grave, and left one of the little blue buckets hanging on a branch as a marker. After successfully crossing the mountain the little party continued on its way, unaware of the fortune swinging in the little blue buckets beneath the wagons. The emigrants had more grief while crossing the Deschutes river. The wagons capsized, the buckets were lost or their contents spilled into the water. Only a few of the little yellow pieces of metal—those the children were playing with or carried in their pockets—were saved.

The party reached northwestern Oregon, settled on homesteads and immediately undertook the task of making a living in the wild, untrammeled west. Several years later, a few of these settlers moved down to Sutter's Fort in California. Here they saw the nuggets recovered by Marshall in the mill race. The nuggets looked just like the little yellow rocks they had picked up in eastern Oregon. Eventually they obtained a few of the little stones from friends who had remained in Oregon, and showed them to their newly made acquaintances in California. They were pronounced pure gold. So much excitement was created by the discovery that a party of 90 persons was immediately organized to return to northwestern Nevada and search for the rich ground that had now become known as the Blue Bucket placer.

Hostile Indians soon put a damper on the party's intentions. The outfit was ambushed, and more than half of the gold seekers were killed. Only two men who knew, or thought they knew, the location of the golden canyon survived to get back to California. These two were members of the original emigrant party. They died shortly afterwards due to hardships suffered on the trip. However, before they died they met and told a Dr. Drane of Yreka, California, the story and gave him specific instructions how to find the canyon in which they had found the nuggets.

Dr. Drane was running a store and hotel and doing some placer mining in addition to his practice, and he was loath to leave his business to travel north. A trapper from the Hudson Bay country on his way to the California goldfields stopped at Yreka. The Doctor showed him some of the gold nuggets that he daily washed out in his sluice boxes. "If that's gold," said the stranger, "I know where there's a pile of it. In a steep walled canyon northeast of here are lots of those yellow stones—some larger, some smaller. A man could load two horses with all they could carry in half a day. Why, you could just pick them up right out of the streambed."

The trapper, it seems, had wintered his horses in the canyon and had found the gold there the following spring when taking out the animals. While the trapper was describing the place, the Doctor recalled the story of the two sick men. According to the description, the two places were identical. The interest of the Doctor grew and grew. Eventually, with two trusted friends and the trapper, he set out to look for the canyon. The trapper backtracked by the dead embers of his campfires. Not until they reached the head of Goose Lake valley did the Doctor know where he was going. From the top of Warner hill the Doctor could see the surrounding country and get his bearings.

The trapper pointed out the two peaks to the northeast about 120 miles away. "There," he said. "That mountain off to the right is the one. The canyon lies on this side and to the north of it. That is where I put my horses out to graze. The creek runs full in the spring and is low in the fall. The canyon is level at the lower end. There is a trail into it and plenty of grass. The upper end is steep. The walls are so close together that it is about all a man can do to get a horse through."

The three men found the place just as described but were doomed to disappointment. A recent cloudburst had played havoc with the canyon. The streambed was piled high with brush, boulders, and sand. The three men looked long and hard, but not a trace of gold could they find. The Doctor never doubted that they were in the right place, but then he might have been wrong. With their food supply almost gone, and being exhausted from their long search, the trio reluctantly gave up.

Some 20 or more years later, in 1879, a boy, G. S. Johnson, and a man, William Adams, were traveling across Oregon. From Malheur lake they headed into and camped at the agency of the Malheur Indian reservation. Adams, an old California miner, liked the looks of the rocks and formations of the country in and around the old agency buildings.

The Malheur reservation at that time was located where Harney, Grant, and Malheur counties join. The agency was located on the southwestern slopes of the Burnt River mountains, west of Beulah and north of Drewsey. At that time white men were not allowed to stay very long on the reservation, or to prospect for minerals.

Johnson remembered a conversation with the agent while camped there. The agent had found piles of old rotten timbers, a grave by a spring and a wide deep track down the mountain about three miles from the agency. The timbers had been used behind wagons for brakes and had cut a large swath or road down the mountainside. Over 50 years later he heard the tale of the Blue Bucket placer and recalled the tale told by the agent.

The story of Johnson should give new hope to the seekers of the Lost Blue Bucket placer. The price is well worth a thorough search of the locality described by the Malheur agent.

MANY OLD SPANISH documents mention the fabulously rich San Pedro silver mine. The yellowed manuscript before me, said upon good authority to have been copied from original Spanish archives reads, in part:

The mine called San Pedro belonged to Tumacacori. It measured one and one half leagues from the side of the mission to the west and when the sun rose over the lofty Santa Ritas it struck in the portal of the tunnel. At the San Pedro mine the rocks are rolled to the canyon. In the mine there will be found planchas de plata (bars of silver) weighing from 25 to 250 pounds each, also deposits containing native silver. From the San Pedro the trail descends to the Guadalupe mine and t[illegible] follows by a canton to the south and reaches the spring of San

Roman. On the west side of the mountain there is a long tunnel with a strong wooden door. Below this tunnel at the foot of the mountain in a canyon running from east to west will be found un vaso (adobe smelter) and piles of slag.

So unfolds the legend of the lost San Pedro mine.

It was many years ago and siesta time at the old Tumacacori mission. Calistro, ancient Opata Indian and self-appointed custodian of the ruins, was sound asleep in the noonday sun. Far across the valley to the east a fleecy cloud hung like a bridal veil from the summit of Old Baldy perched high atop the Santa Rita range. To the west the Tumacacori mountains loomed dark against the western sky.

It was springtime in the green valley of the Santa Cruz and the south wind was redolent with the perfume of blossoms in the nearby orchards and the scent of new-mown hay. Bees droned and great butterflies floated overhead in the warm sunshine. The nearby Santa Cruz river sang a pleasant song as it gurgled among boulders in its rocky bed.

"Yes," replied Calistro, in answer to my question, "I have often passed near the San Pedro mine and many times have I seen strange lights flickering on the high ridge to the west. I have heard that much treasure is buried there."

For a small consideration this old Indian agreed to guide me to the workings. The trail led out across the flats toward the base of the Tumacacori range and despite his 108 years this remarkable old man kept abreast of my saddle mule up hill and down.

After passing the Otero cattle ranch about half way up the mountain the trail swerved to the southwest. Here the formation changed from old andesite to rhyolite, and small stringers of gray quartz began to appear.

A few thousand feet below the summit Calistro paused and with outstretched hand pointed to some large grassy mounds. "Allí hay mucha plata. Búscala." (There lies much silver. Look for it.)

On the summit we stopped to rest and to add a stone to a large mound that marked the site of an ancient grave. It is the custom of Hispano-Arizonans when passing by a grave to add another stone to the pile. As this is the old trail from Arivaca and Cerro Colorado to the Tumacacori mission, many travelers had passed this way and consequently the mound had grown to an immense size. From here the trail wound down to the foothills and out across the plains of Arivaca beyond which stands the magnificent Baboquivari peak which resembles a great eagle with outstretched wings, head and beak projecting into the sky.

A few thousand feet below the summit Calistro paused and with outstretched hand pointed to some large grassy mounds. "*Alli hay mucha plata. Buscala.*" (There lies much silver. Look for it.) With these words the old Indian sat down on a rock and refused to budge. So while Calistro rolled and smoked innumerable cornshuck cigarettes I went on to examine the lost San Pedro mine.

Several outcroppings of gray quartz veins from 18 inches to three feet in width showed considerable copper and silver. There were several grassy mounds that contained lowgrade silver and copper ore that showed evidence of having lain there for several hundred years. The old stopes had caved in and were overgrown with grass and brush to such an extent that it was impossible to make an examination of them. However, several pieces of highgrade were picked up from the surface. Most of the mines in the district are noted for their rich deposits of silver ore. Calistro might have been right when he said "*Alli hay mucha plata.*"

LOST BEAN POT PLACER

THE LATE GEORGE SEARS, an old time desert rat who prospected around Ajo and Gunsight, Pima county, Arizona, for many years, camped one night on the lower end of the long ridge running down from the granite peak just west of the present mining town of Ajo. Returning to camp with an armful of wood that he had gathered to cook his evening meal of sow belly and frijoles, he caught his foot on something and fell, skinning his knees on the sharp rocks. Before gathering up the wood that lay scattered on the hillside where he had fallen, he looked around to see what had tripped him. Near where he had fallen the bales of an old rusty iron bean pot protruded from the rocky ground. Annoyed and angry, he kicked the pot loose and hurled it down the mountain into the squaw tea bushes, then promptly forgot all about the incident until a few years later when he heard this legend of buried gold on the ridge:

Papago Indians living in and around Ajo relate that long before the Americans came to this part of the country the arroyos around the great copper mine at Ajo were worked by the Papagos for placer gold. This seems probable as Ajo copper ore carries a small amount of gold. The erosion of untold centuries carried this gold down the mountainsides and concentrated it as placer on the bottom of the arroyos.

The Papagos established their village near the mines and made their living by panning gold and killing wild game that roamed over the boundless plains below the mines. The country at that time belonged to Mexico, so every year the Papago chief led his people down to Caborca in the Altar district to barter gold for supplies.

The Mexicans discovered the source of the gold and sent an expedition of 500 men to Ajo to dispossess the Papagos and work the mines themselves. They brought provisions and other supplies sufficient to last them for a year before returning to Caborca to market the gold and renew their supplies. Upon arrival of the Mexicans the Indians were forced to abandon the workings. Being a gentle people, they left the mines without a fight.

The Mexicans established their camp in the vicinity and in time managed to take out a considerable amount of gold. After they had worked the placers for a period of five or six months, a large band of Apache Indians on their way from the gulf of Mexico to the Superstition mountains, to gather fruit from the Saguaro cactus there, swooped down upon them from the surrounding mountains. The Mexicans put up a stiff fight but, taken by surprise and virtually unarmed, they were defeated and forced to flee for their lives. So completely were they routed that they had to abandon their dead and all their supplies including a large amount of placer gold, buried in the camp in an old bean pot. Their first stop was at Sonoyta river, about 35 miles south of the mines, from where they finally made their way to Caborca, never to return.

The Papagos who had been forced by the Mexicans to give up the mines were watching the fight from the surrounding hills. The Apaches had made many raids on the Papagos and were their deadly enemies. Seeing that the Mexicans had abandoned the field and fled to Sonora, the Papagos now considered it time for them to act. The Apache warriors were heavily armed, each carrying a long bow and a quiver of arrows, and most of them had large tomahawks under their belts. The Papagos were unarmed. They didn't need any weapons, they believed, for their medicine man carried a buckskin sack full of a mysterious powder that was considered strong medicine for just such an occasion.

This powder, it was believed, when thrown into the air would start a whirlwind that would destroy everything in its path. The chief held up his right hand as a signal for silence. Every warrior stopped in his tracks and remained motionless. The medicine man untied the buckskin sack, took out a large handful of powder and threw it high into the air, just as the warriors let out a blood-curdling war whoop that shook the very hills as it echoed back and forth across the canyons. Almost immediately a great funnel-shaped whirlwind was seen to drop out of the eastern sky and come rushing into the west, headed straight for the Apaches. Nearer and nearer came the great whirlwind, tearing up trees by the roots and bending the greasewoods and sage brush to the ground like blades of grass.

The Papago warriors were leaping down the hillsides toward their ancient enemies who could now be seen standing on a long ridge plainly outlined against the deep blue sky. A large number of women and children, also on pony back, had accompanied the Apache warriors on the trip to the gulf. Frightened almost to death by the hideous yelling of the Indians and the terrible noise of the whirlwind, the ponies stampeded and headed for the tall tules, bucking the squaws and papooses off as they went. The Apache warriors, thunderstruck with fear and superstition, also were having a hard time controlling their horses that were trying frantically to join the others speeding toward the flat country below. The Papago warriors were bearing down upon them from the south and west, yelling like demons, and the great whirlwind advanced out of the east directly toward them. The Apaches were panicky. They decided to abandon the field without a fight, but by the time they got the squaws and papooses picked up and back on their ponies again the yelling Papagos were upon them.

After putting their ancient enemies to flight, the Papagos returned to their old gold diggings where they found enough food and supplies to last them for almost a year. The pot of gold buried by the Mexicans has never been found.

To this day, at the same time every year, the Papagos gather at the village of Moivavi (Many Wells) for a great fiesta celebrating their victories over the Mexicans and Apache warriors. When the fiesta is over and the stars come out, the medicine man gets out the buckskin pouch from its secret hiding place and ties it up again with a strong string to keep it safe and ready for use in case the Apache warriors ever come back again.

LOST MOUNTAIN OF SILVER

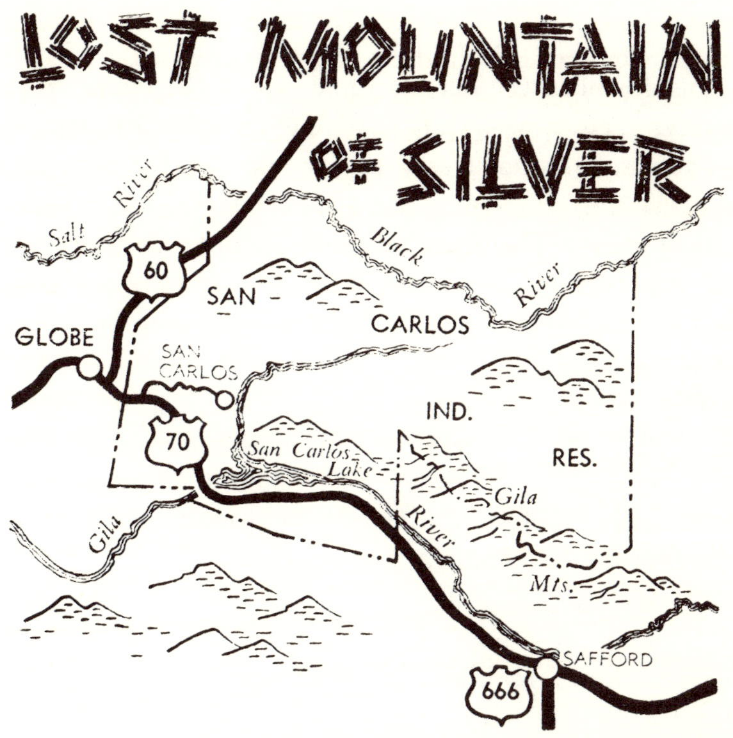

IN THE EARLY SPRING OF 1891, a party of Mexicans from Sonora stopped at San Carlos Indian agency in Arizona. Their leader, Pedro Encinas, said they were searching for a "mountain of silver."

According to Encinas, many years before a veritable mountain of silver had been discovered in Arizona by a relative of his. Large and small nuggets of native silver covered the surface of the ground, the relative had told him, and red, green and black ore veins, rich in highgrade silver, laced the mountain's core.

Age and infirmities had prevented the relative from returning to reap the mountain's treasure, Encinas explained, and on his deathbed the old man had passed the secret along to his family. Pedro was the only one familiar enough with the country to conduct a search. He assembled a party of friends and relatives, told them the relative's story and asked them to join him in finding the fabulous mountain of silver.

With letters of recommendation from the Governor of Sonora, the party started a pack train north and in due time came to San Carlos. They presented the letter to W. J. Ellis, acting Indian agent for the Apaches there, and they were well received. Ellis granted them permission to search for their silver mountain, provided that, should it be found on the reservation, exploitation would be forbidden, and the party must return to Mexico. The adventurers agreed.

L. K. Thompson of the Salt river valley, a brother-in-law of Encinas, accompanied the party. After several days' travel, they came to a mountain which Encinas, from the description that had been given him, pronounced to be the object of their search. Unfortunately, however, it lay within the limits of the San Carlos reservation. Agreeable to their pledge, the Mexicans turned about, resigned to abandon the treasure they believed the hill to hold.

On their way back, they came upon evidence that others, whose presence in the country had been very recent, had not been so scrupulous. Monuments marked claims, small tailing dumps betrayed recent mine workings, and a camp site bore indications of recent occupancy.

A little farther on, the Mexicans came to a stream and decided to make camp beside it. Near their campsite, one of their number, casually exploring the area after supper, came upon a frightful tragedy, the work, undoubtedly, of Apache Indians.

Upon the earth in a makeshift mining camp were impressions of the bodies of several prospectors who had gone to sleep there in fancied security. Cooking utensils, battered as if purposely to destroy their usefulness, a pick and shovel, three cartridge belts and some tattered remnants of clothing lay scattered about. Near the streambed were the remains of a large campfire; in its ashes were partly burned human bones, a sack of corn and the charred remains of three saddles. Nearby lay a canteen partly filled with still fresh water. There was no one about. This was all that was left of a party which had found the silver mountain and had paid for the discovery with their lives.

The Encinas party returned to Mexico without telling anyone the exact location of the silver mountain, and the hill and its presumed riches joined the long list of mines still hidden in the Southwest desert's sands.

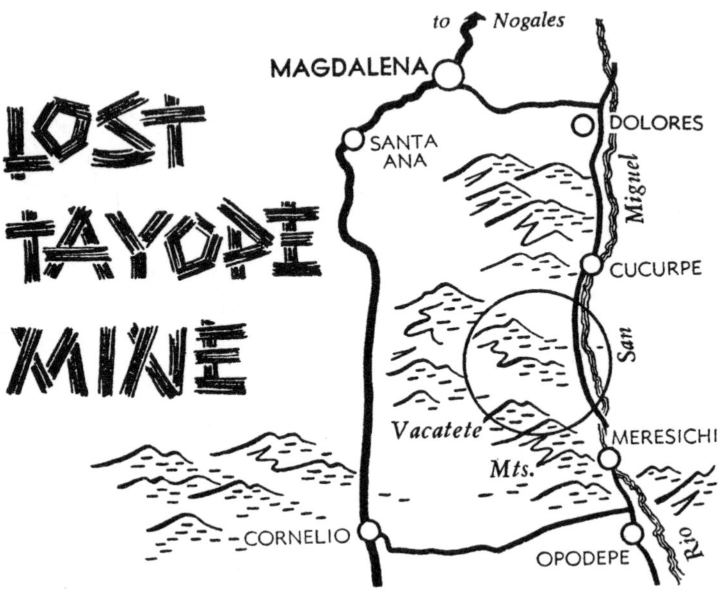

THE LOST TAYOPE MINE was probably one of the richest and most romantic of all the mines worked along the border between the United States and Mexico by the Spanish miners who came into the country in the wake of the Coronado expedition.

Mining men from all over the world have searched the mountains of northern Mexico for this fabulously rich silver mine, now known to be located in the Sahuripa district just north of the Vacatete (Cowteat) mountains in the wild Yaqui Indian country of Sonora, Mexico. Old records indicate that several gold and silver mines were operated in that part of the country during the Spanish occupation, and Tayope was the richest of them all.

The fabulously rich mine was long known to the Eudebe

Indians but was not discovered by the Spaniards until 1703. For a period of 47 years thereafter it produced some of the richest silver ore ever seen on the North American continent. Some of the pieces of native silver were so large that the miners found it difficult to hoist them to the surface with the machinery in use at that time.

As was customary, the Spaniards established a *Real de Minas* at Tayope, and a government official was put in charge to receive the Royal Fifth that belonged to the King of Spain. For a short time after the discovery of the mine, children from Tayope were taken to Arispe to be baptised. Later a church was built at Cucurpe on the San Miguel river, and the padre at Cucurpe looked after the spiritual welfare of the people of Tayope and other villages as far south as Opodepe. The mine is located about 11 miles south of the Cucurpe mission north of the Vacatete mountains and about half way between Cucurpe and Opodepe on the west side of the San Miguel river.

The mine was owned by several people, all of whom became immensely wealthy from its operation; but at the time of Father Pfefferkorn's arrival at Cucurpe in the spring of 1763, they were all in the most abject poverty as a result of Indian raids on their large rancherias and other property. After 17 years of operation one of the owners, Don Bernardo Ortiz, became alarmed at the frequent Indian raids and decided to gather the silver he had hoarded over the years and flee to the Spanish villages on the coast of California. In the possession of Don Bernardo was silver to the value of several million pesos in the form of large balls and slabs just as they had been taken from the mine.

After due consideration and many sleepless nights, Don Bernardo decided to load the great treasure on the backs of mules and into carretas to be transported to the Spanish villages and safety. One nugget of native silver was so large that it could not be carried on a two-wheeled carreta, so two carretas were coupled together, making a four-wheeled ox cart on which the 2700-pound nugget was loaded.

Don Bernardo, riding at the head of the caravan with a trusted *mozo* running at his stirrup, left the mine in the early morning light. The first night's stop was Cucurpe. Don Bernardo and his servants attended early morning mass and at sunup continued on in the direction of the Devil's highway and Arizoniac, a rancheria located just south of the present Arizona-Sonora boundary.

Weeks passed without any word of the progress of the rich caravan. Then one day about three weeks after the caravan's departure, two of Don Bernardo's servants came into Cucurpe and reported that they had been attacked by a large band of Indians in the mountains northeast of Arizoniac. Don Bernardo had been killed by an arrow that had passed entirely through his body; the ox wagon and carretas had been burned and the pack animals stolen. The treasure, in large nuggets and slabs of native silver, was left scattered over the surrounding desert.

In 1730, about ten years after the fight in the pass northeast of the place now known as Arizona ranch, a Spaniard was making his way across the mountains to Tumacacori mission on the Santa Cruz river when he suddenly came upon a large nugget of solid silver. The Spaniard returned to the ranch and notified his friends of his good fortune, and it was not long before a great stampede of treasure-seekers was started. Many people became wealthy from the pieces of silver they found strewn over the countryside.

The Spanish governor of Sonora considered the silver to be a treasure, as there were no veins in the immediate vicinity that could have produced such a large amount of pure silver. Accordingly, he impounded the treasure and notified the king. In due time he received a letter from the Spanish monarch. "The King does not desire to deprive his subjects of that which God has given them," the edict read. So the treasure was returned to the people who had found it.

It is related that one Spanish woman found several large pieces of the silver. One nugget was too large to be carried on one horse, and the woman caused a carriage to be built to transport it to Mexico City. Soon after arriving at the capitol, she was poisoned by the Spanish viceroy who kept the treasure for himself.

History states that one of the nuggets of native silver found at the scene of the massacre weighed 2700 pounds, so there seems to be little doubt that it was the silver taken from Tayope by Don Bernardo. In after years many more of these balls of silver were found and taken to Tumacacori mission and Tubac. Many years ago a prospector showed up at the Connor saloon in Nogales with a burro load of solid silver that he had found in the pass between the Pajarito and El Ruido mountains west of Nogales and just northeast of Planchas de Plata where the treasure was found.

The Opata Indians in the Arivaca country say that before the great revolt of the Pimas in 1750 the Spaniards forced their ancestors to gather a large number of these balls of silver and hide them in a cave in El Ruido mountain. When it was safely stored away, the Indians were killed and left in the cave as *patrones* to guard the treasure. The Indians refuse to go near the place to this day.

The Tayope mine was closed after the great Indian uprising of 1750 and has never been reopened. There are those who claim that the mine was worked out or that the ore was too lowgrade to pay after the rich surface deposits had been exhausted. The old mine is located about 40 miles southeast of Magdalena, Sonora.

When Father Pfefferkorn left the mission at Cucurpe in 1767 on his way to Metape to hear the Jesuit expulsion edict of Spanish King Carlos III, he is said to have buried all the solid altar fixtures of solid silver that were given to the church by one of the wealthy owners of the Tayope mines before he was robbed by the Indians.

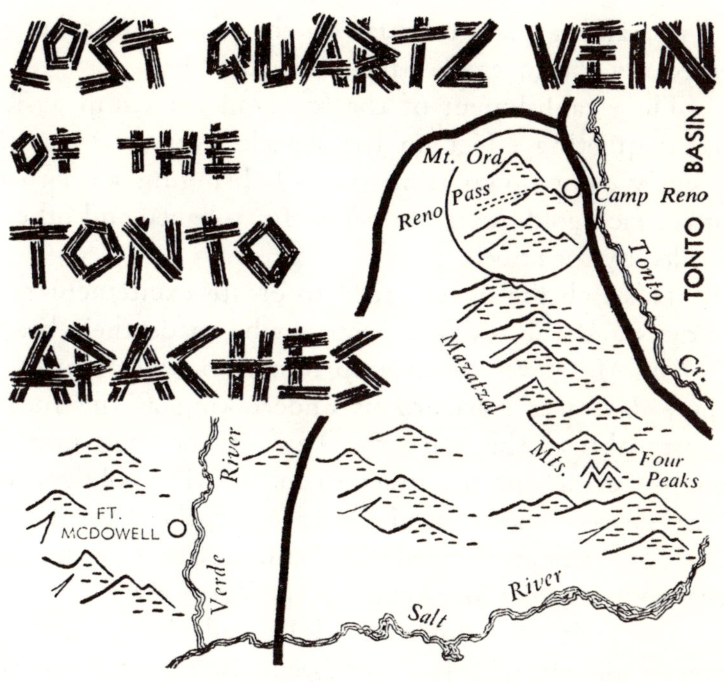

IT HAD LONG BEEN rumored among early day trappers and scouts that the Tonto Apache Indians were in possession of fabulously rich specimens of gold ore, but it was not until 1865, when the United States government established a regular fort at McDowell, 35 miles northeast of Phoenix, Arizona, on the west bank of the Verde river, that pieces of the wonderful ore appeared in the white man's commerce.

Shortly after Fort McDowell was established the government built a military road across the Mazatzal mountains and down into the Tonto basin. There at the foot of Reno pass a sub-station was maintained for several years for the purpose of restraining the activities of the Tonto Apaches — more especially the renegade band under del Shay.

The establishment of the fort and the camp at Reno pass had a quieting effect on the Apache warriors, and they frequently came down from the hills bringing with them pieces of the rich gold quartz to barter for tobacco and other supplies needed by the tribe.

This rich ore never failed to create excitement among the soldiers and the few prospectors who made their headquarters at Fort McDowell and Camp Reno. However, prospecting in those days was a hazardous undertaking as the Indians were constantly on the warpath. Few of the men ever ventured out to search for the precious metal. The soldiers were kept busy chasing the renegades over Apacheland until 1870 when the government decided to abandon Camp Reno and move the troops to Fort McDowell on the Verde river.

On their way down to McDowell the troopers met two young soldiers who had just been discharged from the army. They carried .50-calibre rifles, a supply of ammunition and provisions enough to last them several months. They said they were on their way to the wild Mount Ord country northeast of the fort to search for the Tonto Apache gold mine from whence came the rich ore brought in by the Apache warriors.

The officers from Camp Reno explained to the boys that it was a dangerous undertaking and that the Apache warriors would shoot them on sight if they were caught in the vicinity of the gold mine. The soldiers refused to turn back and were last seen heading into the brush-covered Ord range.

Years passed, but no word ever came out of the rugged hills to indicate the fate of the soldiers. The Indians under Geronimo and other famous leaders continued to raid ranches

They said they were on their way to the wild Mount Ord country northeast of the fort to search for the Tonto Apache gold mine from whence came the rich ore brought into the fort by Apache warriors.

and mining camps until 1886, when they were finally rounded up and placed on reservations.

The names of the boys were forgotten and the mystery of their disappearance unexplained until five years later when two sheepherders driving their flocks down from the hills came upon five skeletons scattered among the rocks on a high ridge on the northern slopes of Mount Ord. Shreds of clothing remained near two of the skeletons and from this clue and information disclosed by examination of teeth and hair, the herders decided that two of the victims had been white men in the uniform of soldiers, and the other three Indians. Empty shells for a .50-calibre rifle were found in the gravel, confirming the conclusion that these were the remains of the soldiers who had gone out to find the Apache gold mine.

While poking around among the bones the sheepherders picked up a large piece of white quartz literally covered with bright yellow gold. Henry Hardt of Chandler, Arizona, lived in the Mount Ord country at the time and saw the specimen. Hardt described it to the writer as being about three inches long, two inches broad and at least one third gold. A ton of such ore at the present price of gold would be worth a fabulous figure.

Many of the old-timers share Hardt's opinion that the boys had found the mine and were on their way out when attacked by the three Indians whose bones were grim evidence of the fight the soldiers put up before their ammunition gave out.

It is a well-known fact among mining men that ore of such great richness seldom occurs in very large quantities. However, a small stringer or pocket of such ore would produce a great fortune for the lucky finder. In recent years Apache wood haulers have been known to bring pieces of this rich ore into Phoenix and Scottsdale. One old Indian described the ore as coming from a white quartz stringer, the eight foot hole being covered over with a packrat nest.

LOST MINE WITH THE IRON DOOR

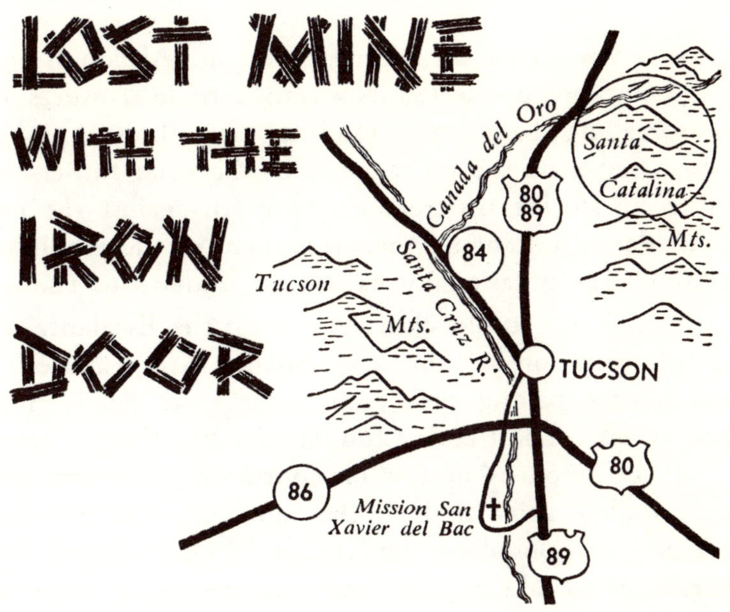

ON A RECENT OUTING in the Santa Catalina mountains near Tucson, Arizona, two employes of nearby Monton Air Base discovered the rusty parts of a blacksmith forge made in Madrid, Spain, and carrying the date, 1757.

The two men knew little about mining and had heard nothing about the Lost Escalante mine made famous by Harold Bell Wright in his novel, *The Mine with the Iron Door*. But their find may be the clue which someday will lead to the rediscovery of this lost Spanish treasure.

The Mine with the Iron Door, as the Escalante has come to be called, is believed to have been found and worked for many years by Father Alferez Juan Bautista de Escalante, a Jesuit priest who at one time was assistant to Father Eusebio Kino at

Mission San Xavier del Bac near Tucson. Although the principal occupation of the Jesuits was to store up treasures in heaven by spreading the gospel among the plains Indians and the wild pagan tribes of the northern hills, the good fathers were not averse to storing up treasures on earth against the proverbial rainy day. In doing so, their treatment of the neophytes under their charge occasionally caused the Indians to rise in revolt.

According to old church records, the Escalante mine was in full operation in 1767 when Spanish King Charles III issued the edict expelling the Jesuit order from Spain and all her possessions. The Jesuits fought the expulsion decree for a number of months, meanwhile continuing to recover gold from the fabulous mine high in the Santa Catalina hills and from placer operations along the Canada del Oro. But they were not permitted to take any of their treasure out of the country.

The Jesuits undoubtedly had foreseen the possibility of their being unable to remove any of the treasure from the country, and they decided to hide it in some secret place until they could return for it in safety. Old Spanish records in possession of Tucson citizens, and Papago legends handed down by word of mouth from father to son, indicate that a large number of Indians were employed in building a hiding place for the treasure. According to reports, the treasure vault was near the south bank of the Canada del Oro. The ruins of the old camp and the foundations of the little chapel where the priests said mass may still be seen.

In June, 1769, while most of the Indian miners and their families were celebrating San Juan's day, a large band of Apache Indians swooped down from the surrounding hills and killed great numbers of Papagos. The mission and most of the houses were almost completely destroyed and were never rebuilt. The mines were abandoned after the raid, and many priests of other outlying missions were killed before they reached the ships waiting to carry them away.

An old Mexican merchant who ran a little grocery store on North Sixth Avenue in Tucson, just north of the present underpass, many years ago had in his possession a faded waybill that purportedly gave directions for finding the Escalante mine. According to this document, the mine was located about one league northwest of the *Ventana*—a natural hole in the rock resembling a window. When the Indian miners stood at the mouth of the tunnel, they could look to the southeast and see through this window.

Old Steve, an Indian *vaquero* who for many years rode the Santa Catalina range, was jogging along on his pinto one windy day when he was startled by a moaning sound coming from a patch of brush near the trail. Investigation proved that the wailing was caused by the wind blowing across a small hole on the side of the high ridge he had been following. The hole turned out to be the entrance to a large tunnel, in places stoped almost to the surface. On the floor were piles of ore that had been broken up and made ready for the pack trip down to the arrastres, evidences of which still stand on the south bank of the Canada del Oro near the ruins of the mission. Great clusters of bats were hanging upside down from the walls and ceiling. Although the old cowpoke talked freely to his Indian and Mexican friends about his find, he refused to take anyone to the site.

Lost mine and buried treasure hunters throughout the Southwest believe that much of the gold found in the Canada del Oro by the Spanish Conquistadores came from the Escalante mine. The heavy rains that fall in the Catalinas every year still wash grains of bright yellow gold down from the hillsides into the Canada del Oro, where it finally settles to bedrock.

The millions of bats that emerge from forgotten mountain tunnels and stopes each evening from April to late October to search for food in the Catalinas, and the accidental discovery of the old Spanish forge high on a windswept ridge may be the clues that eventually will lead someone to the fabulously rich Mine with the Iron Door and to the Jesuits' lost treasure house on the banks of the Canada del Oro.

CAVE OF THE GOLDEN SANDS

FIFTY YEARS AGO, about the time the Salt Lake railroad was being built from Salt Lake City to San Pedro, California, many small mining camps were springing up all along the line and the hills were full of prospectors. An old man with long white whiskers, mounted on a burro and driving four others ahead of him, showed up at the little mining camp of Crescent, Nevada. After watering his burros at the water trough near the windmill he pulled off to one side and made camp. By the time his burros were unpacked and hobbled and the campfire going, Winfield Sherman, Ike Reynolds, Bert Cavanaugh, Jim Wilson and I had gathered around to pass the time of day with the newcomer.

During the conversation, which was carried on mostly by Winfield Sherman, a typical long-haired, bewhiskered desert rat, the old prospector volunteered the information that his name was Riley Hatfield, that he hailed from Raleigh, North Carolina, and that he had come out west on the advice of the family doctor. He said he was headed for Searchlight, Nevada, to purchase provisions and to see a doctor about a heart ailment that had been troubling him.

The old man was very polite, had a good outfit and looked prosperous. However, he did not seem to be much interested in the Crescent camp, despite the buildup we old-timers had given it while sitting around the campfire.

The old man broke camp shortly after breakfast the next morning and by sunup was headed out over the trail in the direction of Searchlight. Two days later I happened to be in Searchlight to pick up mail and provisions and met the prospector at Jack Wheatley's boarding house.

After dinner I joined the old man on the front porch for a smoke and a little chat. During the conversation he told me he had some placer gold for sale and asked me if I knew anyone who would buy it. I referred him to the assay office at either the Duplex or Quartette mine. Late that afternoon he told me he had sold the gold at the Duplex assay office. He reached into his pocket and pulled out five or six of the most beautiful gold nuggets I have ever seen. He said he was sending them to a friend.

I saw the prospector several times the following day, and late that afternoon he told me he had purchased his supplies and had seen a doctor and would be ready to pull out early the next day. He asked me to accompany him as far as Crescent where I had my own camp.

After breakfast the next morning we headed our two pack outfits in the direction of Crescent peak 14 miles west.

About noon we stopped for lunch and to give the burros

a chance to browse. While the bacon was sizzling and the coffee pot was sputtering the old man told me had had discovered four pounds of gold nuggets in a black sand deposit near the Clark mountains northeast of Nippeno (now called Nipton.) He invited me to go with him as he did not like to be out on the desert alone.

He said that one day while camped just below Clark peak, he climbed a short way up the mountainside and saw off to the east a dry lake bed that suddenly filled with water. It looked so real he could see trees along the shore and their reflection in the water.

The route he was following to Crescent and Searchlight was in that general direction so he decided to investigate the lake or whatever it was. As he approached the lake later it had entirely disappeared, and he then realized that it was only a mirage. Fortunately he had brought a good supply of water along. About noon while skirting the western edge of the dry lake bed he saw what seemed to be the entrance to a cave on the east side of a small limestone hill about 50 feet above the level of the dry lake bed.

There is something interesting about a cave. It may contain anything—an ironbound chest full of gold and silver and precious gems, bandit loot, old guns, saddles, artifacts, bones of man or long extinct animals. I sometimes think this love of the cave has been handed down to us by ancient ancestors who lived in caves. When one of those old-timers headed for his cave two jumps ahead of a three-toed whangdoodle the cave looked mighty good.

Likewise this cave looked good to the old prospector, and he decided to make camp and explore it. At least it offered shelter from desert sand storms.

The entrance was a long tunnel. He had not gone far inside when he heard the sound of running water. Returning to the mouth of the cave for a lantern, he made his way back along the narrow entrance and soon came to a great dome-shaped chamber resembling an amphitheatre full of churning water. As he stood there a small whirlpool appeared in the center and suddenly the water rushed out with a roar like thunder. The bottom seemed to have dropped out of the cave. The floor was shaped like a large basin with bench-like terraces or steps that led down to the dark center. The terraces were piled high with black sand that trickled down with the receding water.

Hanging from the ceiling were thousands of beautiful stalactites while other thousands of stalagmites stood up from the floor of the cave. In places they formed massive columns. Around the interior of the cavern were many grottos sparkling with crystals. The walls were plastered with lime carbonate like tapestries studded with diamonds. Never in his life had he seen anything like it. Above the top terrace was a human skeleton and in a nearby grotto were the bones of some extinct animal, probably a ground sloth.

The center of the basin-shaped bottom of the cave was now filled with black sand that had slid down from the surrounding terraces. On the way out he gathered a few handfuls of the sand which later was found to be sprinkled with yellow nuggets that gleamed in the desert sunlight.

According to his story the water in the cavern rises and falls with the ebb and flow of the tides in the Pacific and is active twice every 24 hours. First a rumbling sound like a subterranean cannonading is heard coming from the dark interior and then suddenly the pile of black sand that chokes the tube-like chimney is seen to rise up, and a dark column of water 18 feet in diameter bulges up from the center and reaches a height of 45 or 50 feet. This dome of water and sand spreads out into waves and breaks into white spray as it dashes against the terraces. The play or intense agitation keeps up for several hours and then the pool settles down and is as quiet as a millpond.

If the old man told the truth about the sand in the lake bed and in the cavern, it would be difficult to compute the value of the gold that could be taken from this cave. Then, too, every time the tide comes it brings up more gold. How far the black sand reaches down the underground stream it is impossible to say.

Our dinner was over by the time the old man had finished his story, and we began to break camp.

He invited me to go along with him to his cave and work with him. This I readily agreed to do as soon as I could sell my mining claims in the Crescent camp. The old man promised to be back in about three weeks with more gold at which time I hoped to be ready to accompany him.

I sold my claims to an old French Canadian named Joe Semenec, who was prospecting for a Dr. John Horsky, of Helena, Montana.

The old prospector never returned and to this date no word has ever come out of the desert as to his fate. I have since learned that an old man with long white whiskers was found dead on the dry lake bed near Ivanpah. He and his burros were shot to death. I do not know if this was the same man or not.

The old man had told me that there was from three to six

feet of this heavy black sand on the dry lake bed, which is now covered by a shroud of snow white sand.

Naturally I do not know the exact location of this million dollar cave. If I did I would locate it myself instead of writing this story. This cave should not be confused with one that recently was discovered out on Highway 91 east of San Bernardino, California. This cave is said to extend for a distance of eight miles and to contain a fortune in gold.

Some old prospector or desert rat with a magic lamp to transport him to this hole in the ground could live like a king, if he had enough money to buy a small electric light plant, some rails and an ore car. He could live in a fairy palace with nothing to do but wait for the tide to come in with more gold.

BIG ANTELOPE PLACER

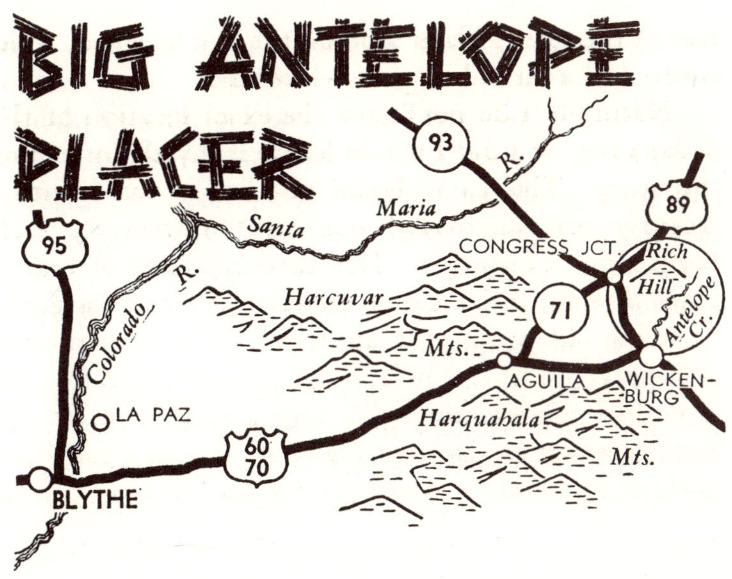

INDIANS ARRIVING AT La Paz on the Colorado river in the early sixties to barter gold for supplies often talked of other and richer deposits of placer to the east. These reports reached the ears of Captain Pauline Weaver and Major A. H. Peeples, who decided to make an investigation. An expedition was soon organized and several days after leaving the mines at La Paz the little party camped at the foot of a high mountain a few miles north of Wickenburg, Arizona.

During the night some of the horses strayed from camp, and the next morning one of the Mexicans was sent out to look for them. In order to get a better view of the surrounding country and if possible locate the missing animals, the Mexican climbed to the summit of the mountain where his attention was attracted to a large number of nuggets scattered over the barren bedrock of the little basin or depression on top of the mountain. The ground was literally covered with gold nuggets that lay sparkling in the morning sunlight.

It is a matter of record that the placer operations at Rich Hill have produced in the neighborhood of $20,000,000 and that many of the nuggets were worth from $500 to $600 each, and some were worth even more. Frequently nuggets of large size were found lodged under the large granite boulders scattered over the mountainside.

A man by the name of Johnson crossed the Colorado river at Yuma with $60,000 worth of nuggets loaded on two pack mules. He stated that he had mined them at Rich Hill and was on his way to California, traveling with a company of soldiers as protection against outlaws and Indians who infested the country at that time.

The Indians around Rich Hill laughed at the miners for wasting their time picking up what the Indians called small nuggets, when only a short distance away in the same country was another mountain known to them as "Big Antelope" where the nuggets were larger and more plentiful. However, the little ones must have looked good to the old timers for they remained to make millions in the big gold rush that followed close on the heels of the first discovery.

It was not until some years later that the hunt for the "Big Antelope" placer got underway. It was about that time that a Negro known locally as "Nigger Ben" and employed by A. H. Peeples on his ranch in Peeples valley, heard the story from an Indian who had been loafing around the ranch. After considerable persuasion he induced the Indian to guide him into the Big Antelope country.

Upon their arrival at Sycamore springs the Indian informed

Upon arrival at Sycamore Springs the Indian told Ben they were close to the gold and advised him to search for it.

Ben that they were close to the gold and advised him to search for it. The Negro knew that there was a superstition that prevented the Indian from taking anyone directly to the mine. To do so, the redskin believed, meant instant death at the hands of the gods or by his own tribe.

While the Indian rested at the little springs the Negro searched the hills for the gold that the red man insisted was near at hand. Failing to find the gold in three days the search was given up and the two men reluctantly returned to the ranch where the Indian disappeared and the Negro resumed his duties as a ranch hand.

Some months later when the Indian again appeared at the ranch, Nigger Ben hired him to make another trip with him into the wild country around Sycamore springs. However, before leaving the second time the Negro advised Peeples, his employer, of his intentions and asked him to send a searching party to Sycamore springs in the event that he did not return to the ranch in a specified time.

Several weeks went by and when the Negro failed to return a searching party was organized and upon arrival at Sycamore springs discovered the body of the Negro. The Indian was nowhere to be found and was never seen again.

Many believe that Nigger Ben found the gold and paid for it with his life when the savage began to realize what he had done, believing as he did that to disclose a tribal secret meant instant death. The body of the Negro was returned to the ranch where it now lies buried under a cairn of stones. The herd of big antelope from which the mountain took its name has long since disappeared and the red man has heard the call of Manitou.

Many others have searched for the Big Antelope placer—but its location remains one of the unsolved mysteries of the Southwest.

OPATA INDIAN SILVER

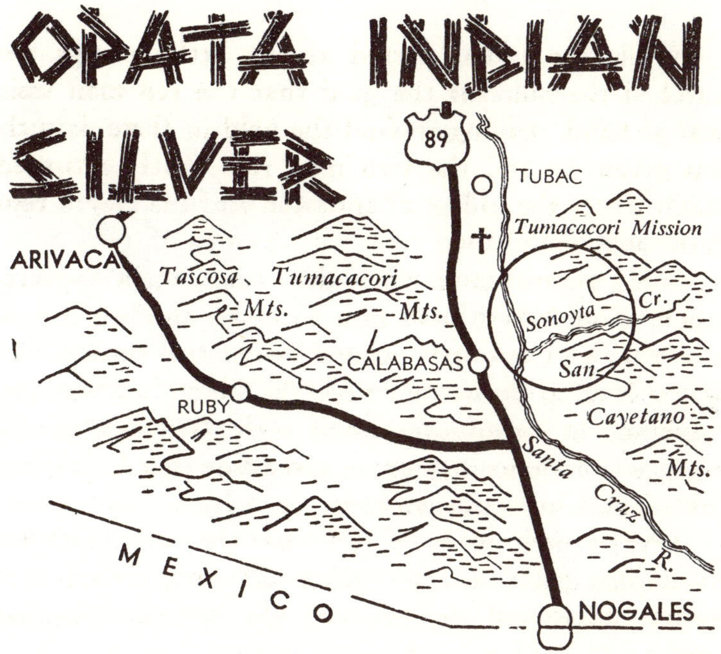

IT HAS LONG BEEN rumored among the Indians and Hispano-Americanos that the Jesuits discovered and for a time worked a rich silver vein in the western foothills of the rugged San Cayetano mountains about three miles southeast of the ancient ruins of San Cayetano de Tumacacori mission, near Tubac, Santa Cruz county, Arizona.

The rich ore was said to have been mined and carried to the adobe furnace on the backs of Pima, Papago and Opata neophytes. All mining ceased in 1772 when the mission was suddenly raided by a band of Apache warriors, and for many years thereafter the old building lay in ruins.

The mine lay idle for 142 years, or until 1914, when it was discovered and worked on a small scale by an old Opata Indian *gambucino* who lived on a small plot of ground on the Santa Cruz river about half way between the ancient mission and Tubac. The old man sold the ore to a Chinese merchant at Tubac.

In 1915, I saw five sacks of the ore in the back room of the little adobe store and had the pleasure of picking up a few pounds of the highgrade and letting it trickle through my fingers back into the sack.

In 1917 a cowman, whose family still resides near Tubac, was riding after cattle in the western foothills of the San Cayetano mountains and from a distance saw the old Opata emerge from a small opening at the base of a little grass-covered hill. The hole was partly obscured by a small catsclaw bush that had grown up in the soft earth of the mine dump. The old Indian carried a small sack which seemed to be very heavy.

Removing a short knotted rope which was tied around the trunk of the catsclaw, he carried it about half way up the hill and carefully concealed it in a clump of bushes. This done he looked in the direction of the old mission ruins, made the sign of the cross and then climbed down into one of the many deep canyons which gash the western foothills of the San Cayetano and made his way slowly past La Cienega, the mission ruins, and thence to his little home beneath the cottonwoods on the western bank of the Santa Cruz.

About six months after the Opata was seen to leave the mine, I spent a month in and around the ancient town of Tubac and the ruins of Tumacacori. Securing board and room at the home of the cowman, I spent some time prospecting the area. During my stay, I heard the story of the lost mine.

The working was an inclined shaft, sunk on a gray quartz vein that followed a diabase dike running in a northeasterly and southwesterly direction across the base of a small round hill. On a clear day when the sun hangs low over the ragged Tascosa and Tumacacori mountains, a traveler may see the small dark opening from the Tucson-Nogales highway.

An examination convinced me that most of the rich ore on the surface had been gouged out by ancient miners. Small fragments of lowgrade ore broken from the gray quartz ledge assayed only 600 ounces silver per ton. About 30 feet down the inclined shaft was a drift to the northeast exposing a small streak of highgrade silver ore assaying 6000 ounces per ton.

Near the entrance to the drift was a small wooden cross and on the floor about half way in was a short length of railroad iron evidently used by the old Opata in freeing the rich silver glance from the gray quartz with which it was associated. The waste and lowgrade ore was dropped down the shaft into the water. The drift showed rich ore all the way along both in the roof and the floor. There were a few small stopes from which the old Opata evidently had gouged out the rich ore.

A map of the district showed that the old mine was located on a Spanish land grant which at that time was in costly litigation, making it impossible to lease. I decided to visit the home of the old *gambucino* and if possible learn more about the mine.

The old miner lived with another ancient Opata whose forefathers had been neophytes at Tumacacori and Guevavi. It was springtime in the verdant valley of the Santa Cruz and while the snow-cap still lingered around the summit of old Baldy high up in the Santa Rita range, the peach trees were in full bloom in the valley below.

Long-haired Calistro was much older than Juan the miner. It is said he had been a soldier under the Mexican patriot Benito

Juarez and had been in the firing squad that executed Maximilian, the puppet emperor.

I found the two old Indians engaged in planting a little garden along the bank of the river. As we stood talking, an old woman clad in a bright new gingham dress came to the door of the little brush house and called out that dinner was ready. In the house, they bade me be seated. Calistro introduced the old lady as *mi esposa* (my wife). When old Juan arrived he also introduced the lady as *mi esposa.* Seeing that I was somewhat puzzled, Calistro explained that they were *companieros* (partners) and went on to explain that the old lady had been with them for many years, cooking their meals, washing their clothes, keeping their pallets dusted and soft and their poor house spick and span.

As the three of us sat on a bench and talked, the old woman was tending an olla full of frijoles and a sputtering coffee pot, and patting out delicious corn tortillas which she baked on the small campfire.

After one of the best meals that I had ever eaten, we moved to the shade of the cottonwoods and talked while the old *companieros* smoked innumerable cigarettes. We conversed about many things, but not once did the Indians mention their rich silver mine. After they had given me their house and all that it contained and shown me such wonderful hospitality I did not have the heart to ask them about the mine, for I knew they preferred to regard its location as a secret.

While eating dinner in the house I could not help but observe that their larder was plentifully supplied with frijoles, potatoes, onions, dried meat, coffee, sugar, long strings of bright red chili pepper and many other things. They had no visible means of support other than the little garden and I felt sure that it was from the rich silver mine that they drew their wealth. Probably the mine has been worked by the family for generations, and the secret handed down by word of mouth from father to son.

Many years have passed since my visit to the modest home of the old *compadres.* More recently I learned that both of them had died, and as there were no children to carry on the mining the entrance to the old shaft probably has become overgrown with desert shrubbery.

The graves of the two old miners are marked with stone cairns and wooden crosses. It has long been the custom among certain Indians to cast a stone upon the grave of a former friend when passing by, and these two cairns have now grown to considerable size.

As far as I know the mine is still a part of the old Spanish land grant, and the owner controls the mineral rights. However, some worthy miner or prospector, looking for a small vein of rich ore, may now be able to make a deal with the owner, now that the litigation is cleared up. The mine will never make a fortune—but it will keep his larder well supplied.

THE POTHOLE PLACER

BUFFALO HUNTERS, trappers, scouts and other frontiersmen always kept a sharp lookout for rich gold deposits on their forays across the great plains and into the mountains of the west.

Early day buffalo hunters and trappers on their way from Deadwood, South Dakota, to Montana, Idaho, Utah and the Spanish settlements on the Pacific coast reported that the Snake Indians of Utah were bartering gold nuggets for supplies, but had refused to disclose the source of their wealth, even to white men who were on friendly terms.

Letters of these early day trappers and hunters to friends in the east reported that the Snake Indians often were seen with buckskin pokes filled with large gold nuggets said to have been washed from the sands and gravels in a secret location by Indian women.

Many years later, Frank Lane, just out of Yale law school, saw one of these letters from a trapper in the West, and decided to do some prospecting in the Snake country before settling down to engage in practice.

Lane chose for his partner another college graduate, who for the purpose of this story we will call John Howard. Together the two men set forth with fresh hearts and high hopes to search for the golden mirage that lay beyond the snow-capped Rocky mountains.

For many months the young eastern college men prospected

in the Colorado Rockies and thoroughly enjoyed their association with trappers, buffalo hunters, scouts and prospectors. Day after day, month after month they combed the rugged mountains in search of pay ore, but beyond the discovery of a few lowgrade gold quartz ledges, they had little success.

Finally the near approach of winter drove them down through the sunset canyons and mountain gorges and out onto the plains of eastern Utah on the border of the Snake Indian country where they established a permanent camp.

Here the inexperienced prospectors had no better success than in the mountains of Colorado, and Lane became discouraged. As spring approached he grew more restless and spent most of his time around camp.

Finally the two tenderfeet moved their camp farther out on the plains and after several days' journey halted their pack mules at the base of a low-lying granite mountain where they pitched their tent for the night. The iron-stained mesas around the great uplift were full of potholes. A heavy rain had fallen and the holes stood full of water. The desert was covered with green grass, making it an ideal camp for both men and beasts.

Howard was pleased with the country and had a hunch that they were going to find the elusive pot of gold for which they had been searching. But Lane grew more restless and decided to turn the outfit over to his partner and return east to take up the practice of law in Boston.

Howard became the sole owner of the outfit, free to live the life he had grown to love. After the departure of his friend he mounted his saddle mule and rode out for a short hunting trip on the surrounding plains.

He bagged an antelope and on his way back to camp stopped at one of the potholes to get a drink for himself and water his mule. The noonday sun was shining directly into the hole and as he stopped to drink he saw some shining pieces of ore at the bottom of the shallow cavity.

He waded into the water and scooped up a handful of the yellow stuff. He knew at once he had found the bonanza for which he and his partner had been searching.

He put the nuggets in his pocket and returned to camp. After a hurried meal he went back to the pothole with a gold pan and worked all afternoon scooping the gravel from the bottom of the hole and panning out the nuggets. As the sun disappeared in a blaze of fire behind the ragged edge of the western ridges, he made his way back to camp with an estimated $700 worth of gold taken from the one shallow hole.

For weeks the lone prospector lived on the game that roamed the plains around his camp and panned the dirt and gravel found on the bottom of the numerous potholes that dotted the iron-stained mesas around the great granite mountain.

When the cold winter winds again came across the plains Howard made his way to the nearest settlement with buckskin bags of gold which later proved to be worth nearly $100,000.

He returned east with his fortune but through bad investments eventually lost much of it. Many years later he tried to return to the scene of his fabulous strike, but either failed to reach the right location or the potholes had been worked out, for he did not find a single nugget of gold.

Old-time cowboys and sheepherders refer to a place in eastern Utah as the "potholes" but none of them has ever been known to pick up nuggets in this region.

According to one version of the lost gold story, the potholes described by Howard were not natural holes such as occur in sandstone formation in many parts of the west, but were excavations made in a gravel conglomerate by the Snake women to obtain the gold mentioned by the early trappers and hunters. If so, a fortune still awaits the prospector who will find that conglomerate deposit.

INDEX